WHERE
THERE'S
HOPE
THERE'S
LIFE

WHERE THERE'S HOPE THERE'S LIFE

WOMEN'S STORIES OF
HOMELESSNESS
AND SURVIVAL

WITH THEOLOGICAL AND
PASTORAL REFLECTIONS

ANTHONY J. GITTINS

Liguori/Triumph
LIGUORI, MISSOURI

Imprimi Potest:
Thomas D. Picton, C.Ss.R.
Provincial, Denver Province
The Redemptorists

Published by Liguori/Triumph
An imprint of Liguori Publications
Liguori, Missouri
www.liguori.org

Library of Congress Cataloging-in-Publication Data

Gittins, Anthony J.
  Where there's hope, there's life : women's stories of homelessness and survival : with theological and pastoral reflections / Anthony J. Gittins.—1st ed.
     p.   cm.
  Includes bibliographical references.
  ISBN-10: 0-7648-1410-9; ISBN-13: 978-0-7648-1410-5
  1. Church work with the homeless. 2. Homelessness—Religious aspects—Christianity. 3. Women—Religious life. 4. Homeless persons—Biography. 5. Homeless persons—Religious life. 6. Poverty—Religious aspects—Christianity. I. Title.
  BV4456.G58 2006
  261.8'325082—dc22   200611199

Excerpt from "Little Gidding" (page 145) is taken from *Four Quartets*, copyright 1942 by T. S. Eliot and renewed 1970 by Esme Valerie Eliot. Reprinted by permission of Hartcourt, Inc.

Liguori Publications, a nonprofit corporation, is an apostolate of the Redemptorists. To learn more about the Redemptorist, visit *redemptorists.com*.

Printed in the United States of America
10 09 08 07 06   5 4 3 2 1
First edition

CONTENTS

Part II
An Outsider History of Homelessness:
Theological and Pastoral Reflections

DEDICATION

The current and past staff of REST
(Residents for Emergency Shelter Transitions)

The women, past and present,
whom the shelter serves,
especially Josie Winn,
who died, frozen, on the street,
and Brenda Graham,
whose death was so violent.

Those who support the work of the shelter,
especially the people
of the parish of St. Anne's,
in Crumpsall, Manchester,
England, and the Spiritan community
in Rahim yar Khan, Pakistan,
who gave so generously,
helping to provide durable and
comfortable beds for everyone.

The proceeds of this book will help to continue the work
of the shelter, by providing fresh, hot food for the women.

INTRODUCTION

Homelessness From the Inside and the Outside

Among the very many people lumped or dumped into a category and then labeled as a social problem (women in prostitution,[1] people with AIDS, sexually abused children, or addicts of every kind) are "the homeless." Sometimes they are the dubious beneficiaries of "do-gooders," victims doubly victimized by condescending treatment or patronizing attitudes. But most homeless people, as a lapel badge of the eighties proclaimed, are "HOMELESS NOT HELPLESS." It is critically important that they find their own voice rather than have to suffer someone else speaking for them. But how can they be heard if nobody listens? How will they ever touch others' lives unless people actually hear their own voices and acknowledge their own experiences?

Even if all their whispered voices were, literally, recorded, and their opinions respectfully gathered, what then? That is the central dilemma that delayed production of this book. Over two decades many homeless women have freely and enthusiastically shared their stories with me, but a privileged white male in a world of deprived and victimized women cannot presume to tell these stories, to speak for the women, or to edit their lives. These stories cry out to be told, unmediated and almost unexpurgated, in the first person. So they remained untold, though lives continued, ended violently, or even began again.

THE BACKGROUND

Inspiration from three sources provided an unexpected focus. First, a reference from the *International Association of Mission Studies* back in 1988. Its *Network for Documentation, Archive and Bibliography* recommended that *IAMS* take seriously oral tradition and oral theology in the pursuit of missiology.[2] As anthropologist/theologian, I was struck by the applicability of this remark to the lives of homeless women. They operate with a very unformalized or informal theology, largely unacknowledged and unstudied by the academy. Yet their experience and wisdom might touch the consciences of people with no personal experience of homelessness, and even contribute to a renewed missionary *praxis*. Their stories might stimulate practical theology: theology that starts with actual life situations, reflects on them in light of contemporary theological (and anthropological) insights, and thereby causes a modification in the pastoral approach and in the minister.

This book is a case study of homelessness that engages with it as a social fact and shows homeless women as real people. The stories are not intended to cause a reader-response provoked by guilt or pity, but to evoke compassionate understanding and social responsibility. Good will alone is never quite enough, so I try to show (part 2) how practical theology suggests an approach, a set of strategies for pastorally concerned people.

A second inspiration occurred in the course of thinking about oral theology and also reading a dissertation[3] that mentioned a book on African church history.[4] One of the editors (Weller) lauds the individual case history approach as a way to understand broad historical trends, since local events are intrinsically significant and cumulatively provide a composite picture. He also advocates looking beyond what he calls the "inner" world of dogma and liturgy for explanations of ecclesial reality: the "outer" world of politics and protest are just as likely to provide enlightenment. The other editor (Ranger) speaks of the need for both outward-looking and inward-looking perspectives. This book is organized with the help of their suggestions, into two complementary sections: part 1 articulates an "inner"—or "insider"—story or experience of homelessness; part 2, an "outer"—or "outsider"—perspective and commentary.[5]

The third contributing reference was a work on self-consciousness.[6] Anthony Cohen talks about the "reflexive self"—the particular, inviolate, very specific aspect of a person. This is a helpful antidote to a tendency to speak of "women" or "the homeless" generically—or "Americans" and other national groups or cultures—as an undifferentiated collective. Cohen speaks of "the irreducibility of the self"[7] as a crucial concept for anyone trying to understand and value individual stories: they are not incompatible with the production of some generalizations, and they certainly help to put flesh and blood on statements that otherwise tend toward the bland or anemic. Part 1 presents a dozen "irreducible selves," demonstrating the impossibility and presumptuousness of speaking of "the homeless" outside of specific contexts and particular cases. To the imaginative reader, these twelve may symbolize the inner core of Jesus' disciples—*the twelve*—called, healed, and commissioned for God's purposes and mission. These stories of real women should leave readers appropriately distressed, disturbed, and determined.

Periodically, over the last few years, a woman has asked about "her" story, fretting that it still has not been published. To the women (since I said their stories *would* be more widely circulated), this is yet one more instance, it seems, of broken or unfulfilled promises. Only recently, the first woman I ever interviewed returned to the shelter, fallen on hard times after years of relative independence. Her first concern was about the fate of her story, recorded and held by me these many years. My decision to ask her for another interview, perhaps involving painful details of her recent history, implied that this work would be completed and that the women's stories would finally see the light.[8]

Part 2 consists of reflections on homelessness, victimization of women, responses of churches and volunteers, the possibility of an integrated pastoral theology, and the shelter where these women have stayed. They were written over several years, and there is a simple reason for including them: although part 1 has its own integrity, the autobiographies are not explicitly related to a wider social or theological context. Part 2 offers that, to stimulate theological reflection and pastoral response.

THE FOREGROUND

The holder of my passport is a "resident alien" (a designation rich in biblical associations, categorizing an underclass for whom Jesus made a public and preferential option).[9] A British national, and trained in anthropology and linguistics, I ministered in West Africa for much of the 1970s among poor (not destitute) people in remote rural communities. Since 1984 I have taught at Catholic Theological Union in Chicago and worked with poor (and destitute) people in the richest country in the world. Given that the United States prides itself on freedom, equality, and greatness (and a Christian heritage), this apposition, not to say opposition, is striking and challenging.

In 1979, a shelter opened in the Uptown Baptist Church in Chicago, with a large room for men, a smaller one for women, and the use of kitchen facilities. Every evening at 8:00 PM, a ragtag and bobtail group filed into the basement where each person grabbed a thin mattress and staked a claim on the cement floor. The space was cramped, the number of people barely legal, and the amenities Spartan.

There was no paid staff; and food—most from the food repository—was prepared and served by volunteers. But it was frozen or canned, and a standard meal would be repeated on successive nights until a consignment was finished: a dozen nights with defrosted chicken *sans* dressing, or canned soup that almost everyone found unappetizing (there were cases on cases of oxtail soup, which almost everyone disliked), did little to lift the spirits of people who lived largely by their wits, were often ignored or abused, and had come to the shelter only hoping to find a decent dinner and a dram of dignity.

After two or three years, another larger facility became available to serve the shelter's needs. The men moved there, and I expected to move with them. But the women asked me to remain with them, arguing that since *they* had taken the trouble to get to know *me*, I should stay! Because I found the women considerably more congenial than the men, I stayed. Those women's stories, with some pastoral and theological reflections and many implicit illustrations of practical theology, constitute this book.

HOMELESSNESS FROM THE INSIDE

"We must review and explore afresh the 'inward-looking'... history." We have many accounts of theology, liturgical experiments, and ritual practice, "yet still only the most shadowy outlines of the inward history," and we remain remarkably ignorant of very many important themes. "We know too little of the existential theology and ritual." In substance, this is the opening of a book already mentioned.[10] Despite some qualitative research, the sentiments remain pertinent, not only to Africa today but to situations much nearer to "home": how little we understand the "inward history" of homeless women and men, or the existential problem of homelessness itself.

This notion (what will consistently be referred to as the "inner history") may help us better attend to the reality of women as they speak of homelessness and many other facets of their lives. Perhaps readers will be enlightened, identify (with) an unfamiliar point of view, and realize more forcefully how the Church and many of its members are perceived.

As Robert Burns said, in his memorably-named poem:

> *Oh wad some Power the giftie gie us*
> *To see oursels as ithers see us!*
> *It wad frae monie a blunder free us*
> *An foolish notion.*[11]

Awareness of "inner history" may provide a new vantage point and free us from many a blunder and foolish notion. Lives have been seriously harmed by the unreflected-upon ministrations of religious people. "Inner history," as used here, is almost the same as H. Richard Niebuhr's usage: it reflects the perspective of the subjects (often victims) rather than those of the commentator (who may have glimpsed their "outer history," but rarely *knew* the subjects intimately).

It is relatively easy to learn *about*, to know *about*, homelessness as a human and social problem. Part 2 identifies some such issues, and that is largely "outer history." The first-person narratives in part 1 vividly represent the "inner history" of homelessness, a dimension and perspective totally missing from the consciousness of those who have never experienced it themselves.[12] Priority is given to this dimension in order to balance the record (due to the overwhelming presentation of "outer histories" of homelessness, homeless people and similar realities), to challenge ourselves (people of faith and Christian practice), to "hear the cries of the poor," and to attend to them and their agendas rather than to foist our own agendas on them or to do nothing.

A CHRISTIAN RESPONSE

Noting that classical philosophers "regarded mercy and pity as pathological emotions" because they involved the provision of *unearned assistance,* religious sociologist Rodney Stark illustrates the point with reference to Plato's removal of the problem of the needy from his ideal state (the *Republic*). He dumped the needy beyond its border, out of sight. Our modern solution is similar: we routinely make needy people invisible, and frequently generalize about the problem, blaming the victims. Stark argues that, despite the prevailing moral climate, "Christianity taught that mercy is one of the primary virtues, and that a merciful God *requires* humanity to be merciful. Perhaps even more revolutionary was the principle that Christian love must extend beyond the boundaries of family and tribe, and even beyond the Christian community."[13]

Committed Christians have a serious responsibility to move beyond *knowing about* social facts, statistics, trends, or problems, even if they are willing to dig deep into their pockets to help; we must, because of our faith, come to know people interpersonally, to glimpse—even to experience—their "inner history." This is neither to patronize them by misplaced charity nor simply to become less naive about the world in which we live. We must be motivated by the same reasons that motivated Jesus.

In Mark's account, Jesus is walking *along the way* and Bartimaeus, a blind beggar, is sitting *by the wayside*. The parallelism seems intentional, and the evangelist shows how parallel lines can actually converge! In a climactic scene, Bartimaeus comes face to face with Jesus, whereupon Jesus says to him: "What do you want me to do for you?" Jesus knows *about* beggars and blindness, and *about* the social fact that the poor are always around. But he is now at a point of intimate encounter that will actually bring him to *know* Bartimaeus as a human being, an "irreducible person." Jesus trusts Bartimaeus and asks him to speak his truth. Jesus does not presume that he knows what is best, but invites Bartimaeus to make that identification himself.

Jesus does not have a set program; his ministry is more a discovery procedure. What he does depends significantly on what people truly need rather than on what he might have predetermined. Bartimaeus epitomizes the voiceless, invisible, generic "poor"; his dignity will be restored a moment before his sight. When Bartimaeus names *restoration* of his sight as his dearest wish, he demonstrates both knowledge (that the Messiah would come to *restore*) and modesty (he asks neither for riches nor fame). He also shows his faith in the one with power to restore both the nation of Israel and the sons and daughters of Abraham. The disciples' initial reaction (repeated so often that it becomes a bad habit) was to marginalize Bartimaeus even more. But Jesus both *stood still* and *called* him. These actions bespeak respect and a desire for encounter. Yet the outcome is not simply "cheap grace," for Bartimaeus *"followed him along the way"* (see Mark 10:52). Parallel lines did converge: but both Jesus and Bartimaeus had to move first. Bartimaeus moved from being *by the wayside* to being *on the way*; Jesus, from a programmatic ministry and the dispensing of God's healing to real engagement and mutuality. Jesus needed to trust; Bartimaeus needed to be trusted.

TWELVE GOOD WOMEN AND MORE

The following stories exist because women were willing to trust and because they felt trusted. We came to know one another slowly, over many years: these are the prerequisites and potentialities of mutuality in ministry.[14]

Tina survived awful violence. Jeanette, too, is a survivor and proud grandmother. Lunette has a dependent son and needs shelter for the winter. Brenda, homeless for half her life, will soon find some respite. Young Darla already has a lifetime of bitter experience. Ranita, determined to survive, sleeps at the shelter where she works. Lisa blames herself for landing in the shelter, but she expects to pull out. Although life for Deborah has been filled with disasters and injustices, she's convinced that "you *gotta* have hope." Another survivor, Janice, has a life filled with peaks and valleys—she falls and gets up time afer time. And so the stories unfold, remarkably different yet awfully similar: variations on a tragic theme. But not all is tragedy or sin: there are traces of comedy and signs of hope. Several women have jobs, mostly part time and seasonal; some are "respectable," and no one would guess the women live at a shelter. Lynette, thirty-seven, has many children, no stable relationship, and a life that mimics her mother's. Janet is one of very few white women in the group. Another is Lorraine, who only became homeless in her seventies.

Other stories are not recounted here, but faces come to mind. Dorothy, attractive and under forty when we met twenty years ago, slid into irreversible dementia and now smiles but never speaks. Every week, nicely dressed and wearing lipstick, she sits at the table but lives in another world. Her mind has gone, but not her appetite: she likes a second hot biscuit with her meal.

Another Dorothy, over seventy, proud, articulate, and professional has been crippled by many ailments and made destitute by hospital bills. I gave her one hundred fifty dollars to secure a small apartment, but that was over two years ago and she avoids me now because she cannot repay.

A Russian woman, Olga, did not smell good and the other women were complaining. She showed me a foot and ankle eaten alive by horrendous gangrene. But she was an illegal immigrant and would not go to the hospital. The last I saw her was when she got out of my car and hobbled across the road on a Zimmer frame.

Josie was weak with hunger. Her hands froze solid to the dumpster outside McDonald's (opposite the shelter) as she tried to get discarded food. It was January, and the city kept her body in cold storage until the thaw. McDonald's installed locks on their dumpsters. But in February we gathered, nearly two hundred strong, and we sang, spontaneously, "The Old Rugged Cross" and "Amazing Grace." After we buried Josie, we went back to the shelter and had a meal of real beef and fresh vegetables and hot bread: a kind of eucharist.[15]

Murleen had the most obscene mouth. But she could be honest and kind: you just never knew which of her schizophrenic *personae* would appear. She had been well educated, and had the most surprising array of facts at her disposal—an *idiot savant* without the *idiot*. But suddenly the *savant* would disappear and the raging *idiot* would generate a tidal wave of invective, and there was nothing anyone could do except wait for it to pass.

Rosalee had a foul mouth too, and a sense of humor. She had been a teacher before mental illness took over. She would reach for a half-forgotten quotation, asking disingenuously whether it wasn't from Act IV of *The Tempest*, or the final act of *King Lear*. When she died we gathered in the church to celebrate her life, recalling the stories—outrageous and touching—of her life. Crazy

Rosalee died long before the stories were recorded. But we also gathered around her *papier-mâché* coffin, remembering her honesty, telling stories of her life. Then we went for another meal, a thanksgiving.

Many women, twelve stories. Stories told and lives lived. Each woman was proud to tell her story, thrilled that someone thought it worth listening to, and longing to see it in print. Each one seemed to experience liberation, catharsis, and great pain as her story unfolded. These are inner, insider histories; they are also *her stories*. They might evoke feelings of horror and outrage in those who read them. May they also evoke action. Someone said, "You repent, not by feeling bad, but by thinking differently."[16] Not only thinking, surely, but doing something about it: Christians should repent by *acting* differently.

THEOLOGY FROM THE OUTSIDE

The relationship between theology and discipleship is the focus of part 2. Authentic theological discourse cannot be confined to classroom or library lest it become "academic" ("hypothetical, not practical, realistic or directly useful"): a dreadful indictment. Every would-be disciple (and theologian) is challenged to seek out conversation, dialogue, and engagement *beyond* classrooms, libraries, and church buildings.

People on the margins of society, whose voices are not commonly heard in theological circles, may have as much to offer as they have to receive. Because they can "tell it like it is," we simply cannot (assuming that we hang around long enough) claim not to have heard the cries of the poor of which the psalmist speaks so often (Psalms 9:12; 34:6; 130:1). God's own poor—the *anawim,* the remnant, the virtually invisible and usually overlooked—can help remove the scales from our eyes and allow us to look into their faces. These are, after all, the faces, in our own time and place, of the very people Jesus privileged in his. They can become the catalyst for our own conversion.

At its heart, ministry is *encounter*. Viktor Frankl was exactly right: to love you must encounter. People of faith must do better than acknowledge "the poor" as a class: we must make the invisible visible, by our encounters. Ministry is also *attending to*. The homeless poor have a human right to the care, compassion, and attentiveness of others. All who desire to be among those others must move beyond notional Christianity; they will soon discover how difficult it is, truly to *encounter others* and to love their neighbor as they love themselves.

In part 2, "Homeless Women and Popular Piety" (chapter 14) explores the world of meaning of the women encountered in part 1. They believe in God and have some faith, but most are unaffiliated with a church. Nevertheless, all people strive to make meaning out of their existence (a critical component of culture), though their interpretations may not be understood or accepted by a wider world. The Church is mandated to go into the whole world and not (simply) to pressure others to conform to itself, so whoever works in the Church's name needs to understand and respect other people's worlds. People without homes are not without culture. An exploration of culture is a contribution to practical theology.

"Practicing Collaborative Ministry" (chapter 15) pursues the theme of practical theology, attempting again to link theology and ministry through a renewal of practice (*praxis*). This might deepen our personal conversion and help us discover more relevant ministry. Practical and theoretical concerns come together in an approach to ministry that could suggest ways for further service to people we might otherwise not encounter.

"Meaning, Faith, and Ministry" (chapter 16) ponders issues of faith-formation and reflection and calls us to become increasingly intentional and reflective as Christian disciples. It suggests how we might find and make meaning in our lives (a prerequisite for a life that is more than just existence, or the passage to death). Theological reflection can be a helpful path to a more integrated life.

"Meals, Memories, and Practical Theology" (chapter 17) is an unconventional reflection on Eucharist. It takes two notions—memory and food sharing—and links them both with Jesus and with the women's shelter, and then leaves the reader to make appropriate connections.

OUTSIDERS AND MISSION-IN-REVERSE[17]

Mission-in-reverse is understood as an essential component of all authentic pastoral ministry and offers both a perspective and an evaluative tool. True ministry shows itself in attending to people so that their own words and actions are acknowledged as intrinsic to an emerging dialogue or friendship. Mission-in-reverse is a delicate undertaking, particularly when pursued among people commonly perceived as insignificant in the world of "respectable" people. But since this is the very perception Jesus encountered, it should yield a harvest of insights for all who venture beyond their own comfort zones in his footsteps. Mission-in-reverse provides a benchmark for authentic ministry, for *mutuality* in ministry. It attempts to address the foundational question: who will minister to the minister? It tries to avoid the spurious charity that wounds the recipient even as it establishes the donor as patronizing and entirely self-sufficient. It is based on an acknowledgment that givers must be receivers and receivers must be granted the dignity and freedom to be givers—perhaps in the coin of honest collaboration or gratitude ("thanks-giving"—which is the meaning of *Eucharist*—or indeed "for-giving" or pardoning the exaggerations of the insensitive donor), which is as authentic and valuable as any other currency.

It might have been Gustavo Gutiérrez, or originally Vincent de Paul, who declared that "the poor are not our problem: we are theirs." Either way, this memorable phrase contains much wisdom. Working among people categorized as "the poor" may provide access to some of this wisdom. And since wisdom is not private property, the chapters of part 2—a taste of working among "the poor"—are offered for anyone with a palate not yet completely jaded.

PART I

An Insider History of Homelessness: Real-Life Stories and Challenges

1

TINA

Earnest and open, Tina is acquainted with grief. Within three years she has lost her oldest brother to cancer, her mother to premature old age, and her only son to a murderer's bullet. She is alone yet indomitable.

Tina's earliest memories are of brokenness and discrimination. She remembers precious little worth cherishing, but easily identifies her shattered dreams. When she was five her parents divorced, and she was shuttled between two homes: one in Texas (where she was born and her father still lives), and the other in Illinois (where she, her mother, and two siblings lived until her mother remarried and everyone moved to Wisconsin). Tina was very close to her mother, but her loyalties were divided because her father always remained part of her life, but her mother's new husband (about whom she is silent) evidently claimed the attention of her mother—attention that Tina desperately wanted and needed.

Her father indulged her. "I used to see him all the time. He would come and get me, give me my allowance, and take me wherever I wanted to go. He'd take me cross-country with him, to lots of places." She was his only child: her two (half) siblings had other fathers.

Her eyes brighten as she remembers something, and she tells

me that her father "was a very nice person. I thought the world of him. And still do. He came to visit me, and left just a week ago." But her memory is bittersweet: he came to visit her, *and he left,* knowing that she was in a shelter! How often was this kind of tale repeated over the years: parents, or siblings, or children would visit, or send a little money to people like Tina, and *then disappear!* It was the story of her life. Her father sends her thirty or forty dollars a month.

This brings to mind another woman, white and in her eighties, who told me—beaming with pride—that *her* son had just sent her forty dollars! She did not know where he was; he did not keep in physical contact with her; but he sent her forty dollars. And he *left his mother on the street*!

Meanwhile, Tina was living with her mother, her mother's new husband, and two siblings, in her maternal grandmother's house. Her grandmother did not seem to love Tina because Tina was dark-skinned, while both siblings were "high yellow" like their grandmother. Tina seems to have been very bewildered and torn, which may partly explain why, by her own account, she never accomplished much and never felt very good, academically or morally. She was not affirmed much or often. Yet she did receive her high-school diploma, which is no small achievement. But she never went to college: and she wears that particular memory like an albatross.

There is no bitterness in Tina, despite her being scarred by life. Her grandmother is dying of cancer now, and Tina is solicitous: the old lady is alone. Only a few moments before, she had said, sadly. "I didn't love her"; now it seems clear that really she does.

"Tell me about your son," I say, gently. She does so, willingly, pouring it out in a torrent, purging herself—and bonding with this virtual stranger, as she goes back to the beginning of her sorry saga. Even back then, her hopes were not very high, and clouds were already gathering over her little life.

"I was eighteen. I had gotten married when I was sixteen. I

was pregnant, and my dad told me I needed to be married. I was a teenager, and this guy was doing all these wonderful things for me." But then things began to deteriorate.

Tina has never been divorced, so technically she has been married for twenty years. "But we were only together for five. He hit me. I left." A pause: "I can't say I ever loved him." She talks about his decline into drugs and crime. "He had not been arrested in his teen years," she says, "but then drugs got into his life, and he started to do bad things. He is in the penitentiary now."

At least she is not being beaten up now: at least, not by him. Yet, although they have been apart for fifteen years, he has not been far from her mind. When her son (whom she believes she loved more than her life) was only five, her husband absconded with him. "He said they were going to the park. It took us two years to locate him." Tina has a way with the pregnant pause, the dramatic twist.

"I found him one day at the library," she says excitedly. "I showed his picture to a lady, and she recognized him! Here, in Chicago: he lived right next to this lady!" The pain in Tina's eyes burns some deep part of me, as I recall another mother, long ago, looking for *her* beloved son, and finding him after three long days.

Tina never regained custody. Such is the lot of people without the varnish of respectability or the veneer of privilege. The police came, she had to return her son; his father was given custody, but his paternal grandmother and her sisters raised him. It only broke Tina's heart once more. She admits, bleakly: "My life was really screwed up by then. So, I let it happen. By the time he came back to me he was a teenager."

Teenage wife and mother, Tina had not had much chance to grow up herself. She recalls the tension between herself, her mother, and her mother's mother. "I didn't want to put pressure on my mother, due to my fighting with my grandmother" (who favored Tina's lighter-skinned siblings). "So, I kinda raised myself. My mom just let me out. But freedom was a bad thing; I had no structure, nobody to say, 'No, Tina, you can't do that!' 'No, Tina, that's not right!'"

Tina is very perceptive. She knows many things that went wrong but feels that she was powerless to prevent her decline and fall. The catastrophe approached in slow motion, inexorably.

"My grandparents had lots of money. I didn't really have to work. I had the good life!" Still, she had strong emotional (though not necessarily healthy) bonds with her mother. "I got my first job when I was fourteen: watering plants. I had many kinds of jobs: lifeguard, babysitter, cleaning laundromats. I cooked for Northwestern University for seven years. That was *wonderful!*" Then her mother became sick and she took time off of work: "It was my mother or my work, and I wasn't ready to neglect my mother."

She remembers the other person she never wanted to neglect: her son. He was five when he was taken from her, though she had lost him for the two previous years. She would not see him again until he was eight.

"I would send money, birthday cakes...and they sent them back. But he never forgot me. Still, he knew his dad was not there ["aunts" raised him], and in his mind he asked: 'What's happened to my mom?' But he didn't have any animosity to me." I note the word *animosity,* notice Tina's assurance, and know how animosity has marked her life so deeply. "Even when he was thirteen, he still knew the number to my grandmother's house, God bless his little soul!" But now her eyes are filling up, and it is not the thirteen-year-old she is seeing in her mind's eye; it is the murdered young adult.

Fighting tears, she continues: "He was very smart, but going through many problems." With insight and honesty she says, "I think that came from me and his dad separating, and him not seeing either of us."

So many children's lives are torn apart as their own parents' had been. History repeats itself. A sense of inevitability pervades these women's stories. There are so many people whose statistical chances of survival, not to say happiness, are miserable-to-virtu-ally-nonexistent.

Tina is also caught in reveries and thoughts—about her son. She never tells me his name. Never once does she utter it. I do not ask: it is the only thing she has, and I have no right to take it from her. "His father was a drug-addict and an alcoholic. I was too—addict and alcoholic." Now she has said it, admitted it, and per-haps purged some of the guilt and shame. As far as Tina is con-cerned, I am not there: she is alone with her memory.

"He was sent to all kinds of private schools. He would go to school and just goof off. He was messing up. He was always ar-rested. He was just not paying attention. He was the only boy in the house of six women. His grandfather was never around. They were all telling him: 'Wear these clothes, don't wear that,' and so on. He didn't want to be there."

A classic story: a disaster is waiting to happen. Tina knows what happened, of course, but as yet I don't. I don't even know how she came to be homeless, which was what I thought we would be talking about. I don't know much about her at all. I don't know anything. And she has never told her story before.

I ask her about her son, how he came to be killed. She wants to talk, to share the burden, maybe redistribute the pain just a little. "It was in January [nine months before], just three weeks after I buried my mother. I was with him three days earlier. He was nearly twenty. He had left home and was staying with differ-ent friends. I've never seen so much of him! He would use mari-juana and stuff. He didn't use alcohol because he would get sick. I couldn't stop him. I tried to tell him what it had done to me. *But he couldn't listen.*" Then she remarks, parenthetically, that his father's family 'spoiled him rotten' and tried to stop him from contacting her. She feels that more contact would have made a difference. She knows she was powerless to change fate, but she also has flashes of brilliant insight: "I don't really think it was the freedom...; it was the restrictions [early in his life, the indulgence-but-with-rules, and later, the peer pressure] that harmed him.

"He was with his friends and was shot in the head. It was gangs...maybe a setup by some girls. He died; he didn't even make it to the hospital. They said my son was in a gang. He told me he wasn't and I really wanted to believe him. He wanted to do something with his life. He was going to join the Navy. But he didn't want to work. He was really spoiled. My dad gave him so much of everything. I wish we had spent more time together...

"I wanted him to get counseling, anything that would open him up a bit. He was real quiet: didn't talk a lot. I think he was lonely. He had a lot of friends, and people loved him, but he was led by the crowd. He did what anyone wanted him to do. People came around him because he got so much. So he was popular." Here speaks the universal mother-philosopher, grieving for a dead son for whom things might have been so very different.

Tina came to the shelter almost immediately after she buried her son. That was not the first time, only the most poignant. When her mother died, she had a ten-thousand-dollar insurance policy, enough to give Tina a new start and a new infusion of hope. She was so exited! But her mother's funeral cost six thousand dollars. Tina says, "She had been there for me and I was there for her. She was my heart and I was her heart." So, not merely from duty but out of love and at great personal cost, Tina laid her mother to rest. Now she could at least look after herself. She had four thousand dollars left. "I was going to use that money for an apartment for me and my son, so that when he came home from the Navy we would be together. It was Monday; on that Wednesday, he got killed. So I used the four thousand dollars to bury my son."

Tina is very distressed. It is as though a Greek tragedy has just been played out in this small room. But Tina wants to continue. I ask: What can she possibly have to look forward to? And amazingly, instead of wallowing, she metaphorically stirs, shakes herself, and sets off on another track, with vigor, focus, and not a trace of self-pity. It is a remarkable sight and an endlessly touching story.

"I can't think of tomorrow. If I wake up, that's a good start! I know that twenty-four hours ago I had a job. Now that's gone; I was terminated. But I can make some money. Enough for clothes and storage... And I do have goals. I would love to go back to school and do nursing ... cooking ... become a chef. But I don't have any support groups around here. If I had a case manager, they could probably find me an SRO (single-room occupancy).[1] Nothing's stopping me from coming over here [to the offices for this interview] to talk to someone."

Ironically, something *was* stopping her: only the previous day she had found a single day's work (day labor), and so had no time to consult with a case manager to help her find housing prospects! Also looming large is the court case dealing with her son's murder. That takes up her time, keeps her deep wounds open, and prevents her from finding housing.

"The only time I'm really scared to death is if I wake up with only a dollar in my pocket...I like to sit in a restaurant and eat. I have no problem spending money like that. My dad used to send an allowance every month, but not anymore. I can always go home to Texas. There's a big house waiting for me, and I'm sure I could find a job. But I go to court for my son."

Tina seemed to have no emotional ties to Texas. But there were other children, age sixteen and eighteen, nearer Chicago. She said nothing about them, their father(s), or their current relationship with her. So how did Tina come to be in the shelter in the first place? She picked up the story somewhere between splitting from her husband and reconnecting with her son. She was on the skids, no longer living with her grandmother, and still in her twenties.

"I was on SSI (Supplemental Security Income) for drug and alcohol abusers, for several years, receiving about five hundred dollars a month.[2] My father would send me money, but I was in an abusive relationship. [My boyfriend] was spending it all on drugs. That went on for three years, with mental and physical abuse."

She talks about the verbal barrages. Words were blunt instruments that she endured continually. She recites the litany: "'c...,'
'b....'; 'you are a piece of s....'; 'ass....'; 'f.....': that sort of thing."
She sounds casual, but really she is very, very tired. Yet she continues, talking increasingly to herself: "I had absolutely no self-
esteem. From never doing nothing with your life...not being 'round
productive people, people doing something with their life. I didn't
need putting down. I was already down from using drugs. But
then someone comes along and says, 'Hey, baby, you look gooood!'
So I think I can have a relationship now, y'know. He wasn't a bad
guy, but he had problems. We were like two magnets. Actually,
we were clean and sober when we met, but we thought we could
'use' together."

She has returned to her first big relationship, with the man
she married. This is the story of the slow collapse of her life. And
her stream of consciousness continues: "The day he hit me and I
didn't walk away—that's when I had real low self-esteem. But I
(already) had low self-esteem when I started using drugs...maybe
fifteen, sixteen years old. My life wasn't a ball. What did I know
about a baby, about being a wife, a mother? I still wanted to hang
out with my girlfriends. My mother-in-law wanted to keep the
baby and I would let him stay with her for days and days....I tried
to work. My grandmother wouldn't help me with babysitting.
The only person who would help was my husband's mother, so I
let it happen."

Tina suddenly perks up, perhaps looking on the brighter side.
"When I was cooking [for seven years] and did have a job, my
self-esteem was high. Now, too, despite everything."

But how can her self-esteem be high now, when she is living
in a shelter? What is her current self-image? She says, "This is my
second time out here on the streets." She speaks when her marriage broke down and her pride would not allow her to seek help.
She uses the word *sickness* of her addiction: she has been in counseling and rehabilitation and she has learned from the programs
and from her own past.

"The first time was when I was on drugs. I was with a guy who was beating me, and I ended up down here. I had other family, but my sickness kept me on the street. That was six years ago. I was doing cocaine, and drinking some." She almost breaks down now as the memories return, and she reveals a perspective on the fear and vulnerability that marks the first-time homeless person.

"The first night, I remember. Oh God! I cried. I felt like the only person in the world. There was no one to help me. I felt so lonely. In that room with all those ladies, but it was like I was the only person there....People were nice to me; a few people. I would talk to one or two. One of the supervisors was Sabrina. I will never forget her."

For almost six years, Tina made it alone. Then her mother died, her son was murdered, and the money and the hope ran out again. She was back in the shelter. That was when she told me her story: a never-ending story.

About five years passed before I saw Tina again. She appeared one night at the shelter—as a volunteer! Things were not great for her, and she still did not have secure housing. There was no time for us to talk. Then six months later we met on the street, and she hugged me like a lost friend. We arranged to meet the following day; she came bounding across the street; we went to McDonald's, and I asked her to bring me up to date on her life. This is what she told me.

"They arrested someone [for her son's murder] but they let him go. Mistaken identity. That was that. Then my husband came out of the penitentiary—and he passed away three years ago, from cancer. It was complications from AIDS. He was forty-one."

Tragedy is the red thread running through Tina's life. But she did have a kind of life for a couple of years before her husband died. They lived in an apartment right across the street from the shelter, visible from McDonald's. Dorothy (attractive, well-dressed, quiet Dorothy) used to live there too, until, as Tina says, "her mind collapsed." Now Dorothy simply smiles but never speaks.

Tina has not had a home since her husband died. "I've been working odd jobs, but not making enough money to pay rent [and buy food as well]. Struggling real hard. I've stayed in shelters, with family, and now in the park. I went back to Texas but that was no good. My brothers and sisters were doing things I didn't like [drugs]. They couldn't help me, or themselves. I was living off of my dad. But I had to leave there.

"How have I managed? Oh God! Through the grace of God. People like you. Jobs I have had. Now the lady on my job has a three-flat. I'm going to look at it this week. She says she won't charge me more than two hundred fifty dollars a month. It's way down on the South Side, but I could still come up here and work. I have six to seven hours' work a day now, and I fill in when people are off. I clean the dining room and stuff, serve coffee, talk to the residents at a facility for seniors. People tell my boss how happy they are to have me, because I make them feel good."

Tina will simply not give up. She goes to meetings, has a women's support group, and another for mothers who have suffered domestic violence. She has been drug-free since a short binge with her husband a year before he died.

Tina is not yet forty-four.

2

JEANETTE

Both of Jeanette's parents are alive, and she thanks God for that. So *why* is she homeless if she has an intact family? Jeanette provides the context for her unfolding story. "I was born and raised here, the fifth daughter of seven children (with sons as the family bookends). I have a seventeen-year-old son and a baby granddaughter."

So, her son made someone pregnant, and Jeanette is evidently close to the child. Her son and his girlfriend are together, and Jeanette "think[s] they will make it." She lives in hope—which is amazing, given her tale of degradation and misery. Jeanette is thirty-eight.

"I had a *very* good childhood. Kinda strict, though. We went to [Baptist] church on Sundays. Now I go to the Uptown Baptist [where the shelter rents space] and the Lutheran church. There were no big problems, no violence and no abuse, when I was a kid. I went to high school and graduated. Then I had a son the following year [she was nearly twenty].

"I am homeless today because I was in an abusive relationship and an abusive marriage. I got pregnant, but I didn't marry my son's father; he's not in my life. He was for eight years, but he got hooked up with drugs. He got help, and now he's doing well.

"After high school I was working, got pregnant, continued

working, and raised my son *to the best of my ability.*" She emphasizes this: whether to exorcise her demons or remind herself of her success. "I had a home; I lived with my parents for seven or eight years. I still have a bedroom in my mom's house, and my son [age seventeen] lives with her."

The boy's father was violent, so Jeanette left him, but her mother raised the boy and let him complete school. "I tell you, that's how God works for me! I was blessed to have parents that are still raising grandkids after raising seven kids of their own. That's the only home [her son] knows."

At twenty-eight, Jeanette got married, leaving her son with her mother; but after three years she left her husband and returned to her mother's house. Even when she was married, she went home periodically, because of the abuse. Life was getting out of control.

"What messed me up? Drugs. Drugs and men. I started getting abused by men before my husband. I thought I was doing pretty well before I got married. I was into my life and my son, and I was watching him grow. I had my parents and brothers and sisters to fall back on. They were all married and out. My older brother is seventeen years older than me, and my sisters are eleven, twelve, and thirteen years older than me. My son's father was actually supporting him financially—until he started doing drugs and alcohol. My son was about seven then. Men and drugs messed me up. It all starts well, but certain things about people irritate other people. So, when I started getting depressed, I would either argue a lot, or smoke marijuana, or drink. The first thing I did was pick up a drink, and black out. I had physical abuse, but also mental. Guys hitting me. One guy pushed me down the stairs. I was on a walker and a back brace."

Jeanette had very little by way of a safety net, except her parents. They were raising her son and she was both ashamed and proud. So she stayed away and tried to make it on her own. She never mentioned her siblings again. I asked how she first came to be at a shelter.

"I'll never forget the first day I became homeless, about three years ago. I was dating another guy—see, it's these guys!—for maybe a year. But the last four months were really abusive. He was going to drag me down the street by my hair. He wanted to kill me. That's why I came to Uptown. He was crazy. *Crazy!* I decided to get my life together. About a month before, my mother told me that she would take care of my son.

"So I left. I had taken so much abuse from this man. He had tried to kill me, and I knew I had to go. I didn't tell my mother. I was dressed so pretty. I had new clothes and everything. Then I took off all my clothes and gave them to my girlfriend. It was forty below zero, Tony! I'll never forget. She just gave me some sandals, gym shoes, a pair of socks, a T-shirt, and some jeans. I called the police and they came and got me at two in the morning. They took me to the station and gave me an 800 number, and I called the Department of Human Services and they picked me up and brought me to the Salvation Army. I stayed downtown while they did the paperwork. They brought me straight to the Uptown Salvation Army, and they referred me to the shelter."

So quick, so efficient, and so routine! How quickly a life can fade away and become a hollowed-out existence from which all traces of human dignity are slowly squeezed out. Jeanette's symbolic stripping of herself and trading of pretty clothes for a nondescript uniform seem to indicate that the spark in her life had already died: she was ready to give up. Though "the system" was efficient in finding her a bed, she was quickly and effectively reduced to a cipher. Each night she would have to register—to show the credentials that marked her as "homeless"—becoming a reluctant recipient of the "charity" that can so easily destroy the last vestiges of self-respect. She was rapidly becoming a statistic.

People frequently left used clothes for me: mostly good clothes, not always practical, perhaps with a little jewelry or a pocketbook. I would bring them to the shelter, but never if they were worn or shabby. The women came to expect good quality and some variety. But many women were unhealthy and overweight, while most of the clothes were for the kinds of people the women may have been once, but were no longer. They chose from clothes that were often a silent reminder of a vanished past, or perhaps of what they had never enjoyed themselves. Even what they liked was rarely their size. Even the choices they wanted to make were almost never available to them. Even the well-intentioned kindness of strangers was another metaphorical slap in the face.

Jeanette remembers that first night vividly. Despite her humiliation and unfamiliarity with everything, she noticed and learned. "O, Tony, when they brought me to the Salvation Army, I was so depressed. But that first night in the shelter, they treated me so well. I saw women of age, of color—and my troubles were nothing compared to them. They *told* me their stories and I was appalled: women abused, with four or five kids, going through the system. I am truly blessed; I can see my son anytime I want. I felt lonely but I found friends. I even feel like I have found family. It's like home. But I do want to get out, to get on, to make something of my life."

Is the human spirit almost unbreakable, or are some people just breathtakingly resilient? Jeanette's fierce purposefulness is amazing. Not only did she get out of the shelter once, her story repeated itself, yet *still* her dreams did not die.

"I got out of the shelter and was clean and sober, and in my own place, for two and a half years. But then....Oh man! I don't know. Coming back. I just felt...kinda strange. I *never* expected to be back here. I expected to be somewhere beyond here. Somewhere I could expand. I do love to be in the shelter, but I have to move on. I have to make all my meetings.[1] I don't have any income, but I am eligible for food stamps." The ultimate indignity: not only shelter living, but food stamps! But she still hopes, and as she talks, her hope burns furiously.

"I've been in Uptown for three years now, and I started volunteering in the Uptown Ministries, Salvation Army, Harper

House, and Sarah's Circle.[2] I help to serve dinner on Sundays and Thursdays. That's because the program I was in [stipulated that] I had to do social work and help people. They're all twelve-step programs.[3] I came here to try to do the best I can, but…you know; it's rough."

How does she look at life, how does she find the strength of purpose to live through the days? As she talks, she shows her "street smarts," survival instinct, and creativity. She has so much that others could profitably learn. "I live…you know. I don't do prostitution. I did at one time—not prostitution really, but I dated men; that's like prostitution. Now I just volunteer. You can get day labor and make money and get free clothes. I don't pay for food or clothes: you can get all that in Uptown. But I volunteer. And when you are in a program, you are entitled to certain things. Everywhere you go in Uptown, Tony, you can get everything you want. But I have a goal: to get me a *real* job: working with kids. I love children. I love people, period! Or telemarketing." She seems unaware of how optimistic she remains, of her humor and lightness of touch (or of the unlikely pairing of "people" and "telemarketing"). She is quite remarkable. The fact that she calls me by name so often, speaks to her directness and readiness to trust, even after so many tribulations.

Jeanette is very presentable—clean, well-dressed and cheerful—and I say as much. Suddenly she is self-conscious, a little embarrassed: "Oh Tony, cut it out!…but yes!, that's important in my life. I'm always wearing real pretty clothes. That's probably my personality. I've always loved to dress: that keeps me going." Thank God for everyone who leaves clean clothes for the shelter.

What are Jeanette's memories, good or bad? She jumps right in, and it is not immediately clear which kind she's talking about. "Probably now. Seriously, Tony. Because I'm happy now. It's much smoother. I'm with a person who really cares for me and I know he won't hurt me. I've known him for three years. We don't have a "relationship": communication is the best relationship in the world. We keep it strong by talking and being honest. That's what

I never could do with anyone else. I never knew someone who could listen to me and talk to me: let me know how you feel and I'll let you know how I feel. We don't keep anything away from each other. If you can talk it's the best friendship to have. He's in the People's Church [Shelter]. We support each other a lot.

"My worst memory? When I was beat up. When he tried to kill me. That was the worst time of my life. I'd never had anyone do that to me. My *father* never did that to me! My father never even hit me; my mom did all that, all the abusing and whipping and that stuff. You know what? When I was younger I would say, 'my mom is just so mean,' but when I grew up I knew it was for the best and I thank God for her. She whupped me 'cos I was so bad. I must of been bad because she really whupped me a lot. But I deserved every one of them, 'cos I see today...I would lie; tell stories."

Beatings from Jeanette's man and from her mother have merged. She blames herself for some of what happened to her ("I must [have] been bad..."). But now she wants to talk about another kind of abuse: abuse from the very system that is designed to protect citizens.

"I've been harassed by the police! I've been arrested two or three times. I've been incarcerated three times since I've been in Uptown. Maybe for an hour, or two hours. The first time I saw a judge he said, 'Miss White, why did you wait thirty-seven years to be arrested?' They pinned me on soliciting. They ran me in the computer. They ran my fingerprints. Everything was clear, but still they took me in. It was police harassment. They dropped the charge."

How does she continue to fight? Does she have anything still in reserve? In fact she hasn't really begun to touch the depths of her struggle yet. It turns out that the dark cloud of the arrest had a silver lining: she was referred to REST—the agency responsible for the shelter and programs for homeless people.

"So, I was referred here. They got me a case manager. They said that to get in the program you had to be either an alcoholic or a drug addict, and I was both. I did ninety meetings in ninety days. But I've done one hundred eighty meetings in ninety days. The first eight months in Uptown, I was clean and sober. I never had a problem with the program. I loved it, Tony! I loved it! Until I got hooked up with someone else. Then it really destroyed my life. I had had housing for two and a half years until I broke my foot—I'll get to that. I was in the Northmere.[4] I had privileges. I could have visitors. Then I wanted cooking facilities, so they moved me to the Sheridan, right around the corner from the shelter, for a year. I did a 180/90. I ended up chairing the meetings; that's how much 'clean time' I had. Then I fell again. I met someone. He didn't use and I didn't use. We went through the whole program together. We dated for two years and had a good relationship. Until he started drinking. Then I started drinking. And the whole cycle started again. We had stayed away from people drinking. We had been careful. We knew the dangers. But...I'm back in the program now. They are giving me another chance."

One thinks of the conventional theological language of conversion, of the cheap bromides we dispense: that we must repent, make a firm purpose of amendment, begin again, never give up, trust in God... But here, without a trace of rancor or self-justification, was a woman who had been *living* conversion day after day, with so little help from friends, or Church. To have done one hundred eighty meetings in ninety days, then to have slipped, and yet to have begun again! Elie Wiesel said that only God has power to begin, but we have been given power to begin again, and again. Jeanette was a memorable example of someone who demonstrated that this was indeed possible, though so very costly.

"Last year I broke my foot. I fell down three flights of stairs and when I hit the bottom I hit a steel plate. All the bones in my heel were broken. I'd gotten my heel caught in a rug, and I fell straight down. I fractured my back and had to wear a back brace, and use a walker. So I had to go back home again...for three months. I've been in the shelter now for eight months [with an orthopedic shoe and a back brace]."

How does Jeanette feel: about herself and the world and maybe God? She talks about herself, about "respectable people" and about her longer-term goals. God will come later. "I feel good about myself. I've always felt good about myself. That comes from other people who support and love me. All kinds of people. I wouldn't be able to survive without that. Support from the people of Alcoholics and Narcotics Anonymous, but above all from all the homeless people. They support me.

"You know, they ['respectable' people] help you too! All these organizations I go to have people who come out and show their love for the homeless. And I love that more than anything—*people who come out and tell us they care*. We care about them for doing it. Sometimes there are people who are not that kind. But I can't focus on that. I have to focus on the good things; if I focus on the bad I will be so depressed and feel so sorry for myself. No! I have to do it one day at a time. I would like a good job and a husband. I would like to watch my granddaughter grow, and my son. Oh God! She's beautiful!"

Jeanette previously alluded briefly to the "sex trade." How important is sex in her life now? She is very candid and dignified: "You *could* do without it, yes. But you really don't want to do without it. I wouldn't want to live without it, but it's not a big part of my life. It's not worth it when there is violence and abuse. That's not worth it. Nothing's worth that. If sex is going to hurt you, don't have it….But you never know until it's too late. But there *are* good men in the world. I know that. I think I've finally found one. I have, Tony! He's a nice guy. He's not abusive to me. He's never been married, never hit a woman in his life, he says. And I believe him. Whatever I say, it's OK with him, so long as we are together. He wants to tell you his story. A couple of guys want to tell you their story, Tony. We tell them we're going to Tony to tell him about our lives and our past and that. They say, 'we would like to meet a guy like that.'"

And so stories continue to be told and to affect lives. Theology is largely story, and many stories are the raw narrative form of theology. Jeanette and her friend, her man—each living in a different shelter—try to make it on the streets and through life's tortuous pathways. They try to live out a story, in hopes, surely, of a "happy ever after." But those of us who have been privileged to hear, perhaps even to be shocked by, the stories, what of us? Will we simply forget, or will our own stories extend by the addition of another chapter—perhaps about our own ongoing conversion to God, and to God's poor?

3

LUNETTE

It is mid-November and a raw wind screams off Lake Michigan. Winter is fast approaching, and Chicago winters are unforgiving. Lunette is only a little older than Tina or Jeanette, but looks considerably older. She had only recently become homeless and still seems to be in shock. She prides herself on being a God-fearing woman, but her recent experiences have placed a strain on her relationship with God.

We sit in a small, quiet room, and she is eager to talk. Like many of the women, Lunette actually seems to feel privileged by this opportunity to be interviewed. They feel they have won something, like the lottery. And though their stories are not those of the conventional winners, their enthusiasm attests to how much people like to be listened to and affirmed. Lunette begins her tale.

"My name is Lunette Crockett. I was born and raised in Alabama, and I graduated from high school. My momma brought me up in the Baptist church. I have six sisters and four brothers. My parents are deceased and I have been in Chicago for twenty-nine years."

Lunette is neat and organized in thought and deportment. Her speech is as precise as her body language: controlled, mannered, deliberate. She continues. "My parents were always together. My brothers and sisters [from forty-five to sixty-four years old; she is close to fifty] are all over, but I have two sisters in Chicago, and a twenty-two-year-old son. My husband is deceased. Both me and my son are in the shelter.[1] We are trying to find a place to live, before it gets too cold."

She seems an unlikely person to be in a shelter—though homelessness is an affliction that can befall some of the most unlikely people. What was it like that first night?

"It was real scary when I first came. This past August [two months previously] was the first time I had ever been in a shelter, ever been homeless. Before that my son and me were in an apartment on the South Side. The landlady had rent problems with the other tenants, but every month I paid two hundred fifty dollars. I was the only one paying rent. But she evicted everyone. She evicted me illegally. She just threw me out with the rest. I can sue her when I get a place of my own. DHS [Department of Human Services] brought me to Uptown. They asked why I got evicted. Then they brought both of us to the shelters. It's very, very scary coming to a shelter. My son don't want to be in one, because he ain't never been in a shelter before. I cried for two days. It's real scary. At first I didn't want to have nothing to do with the people at the shelter. It was just real frightening, being out on the streets. Both the shelter and the street. Just the idea of me being in a shelter and being homeless...I never been homeless before. That's the really scary part."

Plaintive and panicky, Lunette loses her composure and her grammar: however much she wants to talk and needs someone to listen to and receive her story, she is also feeling humiliated—and talking to a virtual stranger. The dam bursts and she cries out in pain: "I felt angry, because I knew it was no fault of mine being in the shelter. I really was scared, scared of being out on the streets."[2] Later she will talk about God and the Church. But now she shifts gears and begins to talk about transitions, about people in general, and about her family.

"I've found an apartment, but I can't get it because I have not been able to contact the janitor. I'm going to keep calling until I get that apartment. Here at REST they are going to help me. I've met a whole lot of real nice people. The women are very nice—but some are scary, or frightened. They all want a place to stay. They all want to leave. They are just scared for everybody. People get beaten up. The police: some are good and some are bad. They arrive, but it's always too late! You never know, when they come, whether you will be talking to the good ones or the bad ones. So you just try to manage on your own, before you call a cop.

"I have one older [and one younger] sister in Chicago. I called her when I first got kicked out. I asked her if I could come and stay with her. She told me, to my face, that she didn't have any room for me. I was hurt; real hurt. I felt lower than a snake, the way my sister told me that. I did not expect that from her. My other brothers and sisters know. My sister in Indiana said that if I went there looking for an apartment she would help me look. But I don't want to go to Indiana. It's so quiet there, and I've been in Chicago so long. I've gotten used to the noise. If I were somewhere quiet I think I'd go crazy."

It is difficult to fathom how so large a family of siblings can fail to help its neediest. But Lunette's integrity shines through: she will not go somewhere she does not know, even with her sister's facile promise; better the Chicago you know than the Indiana you don't. And what about her daily routine, her hopes?

"I go to Sarah's Circle, the Salvation Army, Harper House. I am looking for my apartment. I try to keep myself busy. I don't want to be thinking about what's happened to me. I don't want to feel sorry for myself, because I never have in the past. I just don't want to start crying! I have to keep strong. I talk to God.

"My son is twenty-two. He helps with senior citizens at church. He picks them up and takes them home again. At Christmas he helps them, goes shopping for them, and if someone needs their house cleaned up he'll go do it. I see him every day. He goes to Truman College. He has a part-time job that helps him pay for that. He has a high-school diploma. Me too. He worked at Jewel [grocery store] in Palatine, Illinois. We used to live there about two years ago. He passed his driver's test. But he needs glasses. He didn't pass that part of the test. He doesn't bear a grudge against anybody. He's always been happy."

And his mother, clearly, is proud of him and bursting to tell someone! He must have got some of his civic and religious spirit from her, because later in the conversation she would say: "I don't got no animosity toward people with cars and jobs and homes. Maybe because of the way I was brought up. My momma told us not to hold a grudge against anyone. And people ['respectable' people] on the streets are fine, too. They're not mean. I don't beg from them. I have my LINK card and my check. I have enough to live on.[3] If I see someone on the street who is in trouble, I would help them out. I will lend a helping hand. I share with them. People on the street, sometimes they look after one another, and sometimes they don't. There are more men on the street. They can survive better. I have a card, so I can get into the shelter every night, no questions asked. I'm not in the lottery, because I have a card.[4] Cardholders are never in the lottery. I come and talk to the case manager. To keep the card you have to come to the case manager's meeting once a week. But there is art, therapy, AA, and NA. I go to them [voluntarily, socially]. They have a community there. You can play bingo too. I go to the AA meetings to keep myself busy. Also, I want to know how come so many people are on alcohol or cocaine. I want to know why. Some of them don't get the help to get off. They need to get the help, but they don't get it. They need counselors and sponsors."

Lunette is socially aware, self-aware, and attentive to the world she lives in. She has an intuitive sense of the need for community, not only for herself but for others who may benefit from her presence. She *contributes* at least as much as she receives. She is a remarkable woman in any circumstances: in the circumstances in which she finds herself, she is heroic. As for the future, she has a healthy hope: "I look forward to going back to church, to being with my church family. I want to die a happy death, and I know I'm going to live forever in paradise. I don't worry about death, dying, or a funeral. My son will look after that. I got insurance, and I want to start paying for my funeral. Getting an apartment and paying for my funeral are equally important to me. I want to be in an apartment before Thanksgiving [less than three weeks away]. I really believe it will happen, because I believe in God. Even if I don't have a place by Thanksgiving I will still feel the same way about God."

Will she talk about the best of times and the worst of times, I ask, and can she say how she would like to be remembered, whether at the funeral she is so healthily concerned about, or afterwards, in the memories of her son and others? The words tumble out of her mouth, as though they have been waiting for the opportunity to be born in this warm, quiet, safe environment.

"The worst thing by far is being on the streets! The fear. I been lucky, I ain't never been abused." The fear of that possibility is in her every word. She will not use a word stronger or more explicit than "abuse/abused," but clearly she fears rape and other forms of violence. Even her grammatical control slips as she tries to regain some poise. "Me and my son be together every day, until he go to school. Manicure[ist]. He wants to go be a male nurse later. I'm proud of my child."

Can she think of better days, behind, and perhaps ahead of her? "When I was growing up, O! I had some *good* times! It wa'nt like it is now. It's crazy to me these days. I had good times. I had fun. I did things and I kept myself out of trouble. And me and my mom did things together. We went to church. We shopped. And we had a farm. My mom and dad were the best people in my life. They raised eleven kids without putting us on welfare. We had a small farm. Chickens and pigs and cows and horses. And we raised our food.

"How would I like to be remembered? Like I am. I'm always happy. I'm friendly with people. I get along with people. I can get along with anyone. My mom always taught me how to treat other people: if you treat them nice they will treat you nice. There was a whole lot of racism when I was growing up. But my mom, she taught us not to be racist. I have nothing against no white people, because my mom taught us."

Her graciousness and big-heartedness are very impressive. How does she respond when white folk (particularly at the shelter) *are* racist? Without a speck of condescension she says: "I pray for them. 'Cos they don't know what they're doin'. They are ignorant. They teach their kids the same way. I feel good about myself. When I get my own place I will come back to the shelter and help them."

I often leave these interviews, talking to myself, asking myself how people can possibly have such strength of character, and finding myself wanting: wanting to learn from women like Lunette, hoping there is still time. But still, how could those siblings allow her to fall between the cracks? I can still catch the fear underneath Lunette's courage. I wonder what would happen if she lost her son. Tina did.

4

BRENDA

B renda was almost thirty-five when she shared her story, and she never really finished it. Brenda had a complete family, but a very small one. The only child of parents who (she says) were devoted to each other, Brenda's mother died when she was only nine. Both parents were only children, and Brenda felt very alone without aunts or uncles, sisters or brothers, nephews or nieces: only Brenda and her father. Her mother died in her sleep, perhaps a merciful release, since she was addicted to alcohol and "nerve" pills. So, did Brenda salvage a happy childhood?

"No, I didn't. Pretty boring. Being an only child, I had everything a little girl could want. But I never played with things. I took things and threw them away. My father used to yell at me, telling me I didn't appreciate anything. He was an alcoholic too. He passed away when I was twenty-five."

That was about nine years ago. But Brenda had already struck out on her own, leaving home—and father—when she was sixteen, having discovered that she was pregnant. Indignity built on indignity, for it was her father who told her to leave. Since then, for almost twenty years, Brenda has lived on the streets and in shelters. She tries to smile, but it does not come easy. Nothing does, in these dark days.

"When I was pregnant, I went to a battered women's place

because the guy I was going with was beating up on me when he found out I was pregnant. He started fighting me then: some guys are jealous. This guy wanted me to have an abortion. I chose not to."

Several times, very deliberately, Brenda says that she "chose not to," or "chose to" do something. Psychotherapist Viktor Frankl once said: "To live you must choose." Ironically, Brenda chooses but never seems to have much of a life.

"Well, we ended up still going together. Then you could get a [public aid] check when you were pregnant. He used to jump on me because I wouldn't give him my money. He took my money from me. That was the first time I got a black eye. He knocked me out cold. I had been going with him since I was thirteen. He started getting abusive two years later [about when she got pregnant], but not at first. When I had my baby—my son—I escaped. I was staying at the shelter 'til I had my baby.[1] My boyfriend was in jail for beating me while I was pregnant. We had been just hanging around. He didn't have a job. But I had done all my twelve years in school."

It sounds as though she had struggled and almost made it. But her life was much more complicated than one could ever have imagined.

"The actual moment I graduated I started in labor. That was my third child; I was pregnant three times in high school. I went into labor as I was walking across the stage, and they took me straight from the graduation ceremony to the hospital. The other two times I was also staying in a women's shelter. They took care of me until I was eighteen. I had three babies then. So, when I had the first I was in the battered women's shelter [Rainbow Light]. The first year was hard because I didn't know anything about kids. I got some day-labor work. They had a daycare center and they watched the babies for me. When I was eighteen, they sent me to the Salvation Army. I got my first apartment then. I got public aid and saved up four hundred dollars, so I got my apartment. I had gotten pregnant seven months after my son's birth. I met this guy, Roy. We were together, but I choose (*sic*) not to live with another guy."

Brenda explains that she was with Roy, as companion and caretaker on the streets, but that they did not have an ongoing sexual relationship after becoming pregnant. She stayed in a shelter for two years, and Roy actually looked after her two children, a boy and a girl. She says, very deliberately, that she "chooses" to do certain things, using the present tense. It is clear that she places certain expectations upon herself, and that she has become quite intentional about as much of her life as she feels able to control: so she chooses.

"I was working during the [third] pregnancy. He wanted me to quit but I choose not to. He was with me all through the pregnancy. He was working. We stayed together for eight years. He is the father of the second, third, and fourth kids. Three months after my daughter, I got pregnant with my other son." So much for "choosing" not to have an intimate relationship. She is candid about the circumstances of her life, and acknowledges that she was—like many other women who talked about their experience—terribly naive. "I was kinda' tripping because I was having babies too fast. My father had not told me anything about birth control or anything. I had to find that out on my own. After my third child, I went and got myself some birth control pills." She repeats the story of her graduation and going into labor, adding the touching fact that both the father of her child and her own natural father were there—and presumably at the hospital immediately afterwards.

"After that, Roy and my father didn't get along too well. My father thought he was too 'fast.' He called me out by name. That was abusive. He called me 'red bitch,' 'tramp,' and so on. He was light skinned and my mother was light skinned. When he died, we were in, like, a bad relationship. Anyway, when he passed I ended up in the shelter with my three kids. I buried him. He had insurance for that, but there was nothing left over for me."

Despite her cheerful determination to survive and to succeed,

Brenda has needed to make some serious decisions. What else did she decide *not* to do, and at what cost? When she got pregnant for the third time—only three months after giving birth to her second child, and still many months away from graduation—why did she not get an abortion?

"I couldn't afford it then. Anyways, I don't really think I would have. I always said to myself that being an only child, I would want my own children to have brothers and sisters."

Looking at Brenda's current circumstances, it is difficult to grasp the conviction with which she talks of this priority: her children do indeed have siblings, yet there is no family in a conventional sense, her life is far from stabilized, and now she has three motherless children! Brenda is very warm and evidently well-intentioned, and with a little probing, she will disclose the "inner history" that holds the key to her life story.

What part, if any, has religion played in her life? How did her post-school life start to fall apart? She hardly pauses, and seems very, very honest.

"I've had religion. I was baptized five or six times. Because I'm a 'backslider.' There were different churches. Baptist churches. When I was seventeen my counselor got me [back] to church. I never had any church with my parents. My parents drank. They argued and fought all the time. There was lots of abuse: the noise. Still today I jump at the noise. My worst memories are of my father and mother fighting a lot. They beat up on each other. I used to go and hide…in the closet. They didn't beat me. I went to school and [did] everything they told me. But they never sat down and talked to me. They gave me everything a little girl could want, but like, 'take this, and go over there,' or 'to your room'. They gave me things—coloring books, toys—but never instructions or advice. Everything I know, I learned on my own, through being on the streets."

Brenda was taught little of enduring value, either at school or at home. At least, she seems to have *learned* very little. But in school, peer learning evidently contributed to her multiple pregnancies.

Meanwhile, at home, starvation of affection seems to have made her very vulnerable to sweet-talking boys. Her parents seem to have been so self-absorbed that they did not even teach her the facts of life, and though she discovered the mechanics she was evidently very immature emotionally. By the time she picked up some practical assistance it was already too late. As she continues, she seems to drift away into another world, her language losing its crispness and softening into the more familiar cadences of African American English.

"[Still at school], when I was pregnant the third time, I mixed with people more, and talked more—to counselors and such. During the first two [pregnancies] I kept to myself. But now I was in the shelter. I wanted to go to college. The babies' father was still with me, so we decided to get an apartment: The Robert Taylor Homes.[2] This is 1984. But when my baby was eight months old, that's when I got introduced to drugs. I met this girl. I was, like, a social drinker: I might drink a beer. We were sitting in the kitchen one day, and she came in with this white powder. I said, 'What you doin' with that?' and she said, 'Oh girl, you never tried this? It make you feel good.' I tried it but I didn't feel nothin'. But these people, they want to get you strung out on drugs. They give it to you free. But once you get used to usin' the drug, you got to pay for it. I ended up gettin' hooked on it. I was neglectin' my children and spendin' my whole [public aid] check. That didn't last long. And sometimes people would come to my house [for drugs]. Within six months I was completely neglectin' my children, I had stopped payin' rent, I was sellin' the food stamps, was strung out—and started sellin' my body. My man was working and he didn't know I was doing all this behind his back. You can make, oh, two hundred or three hunded dollas a day if you just stay out there. I felt bad about myself, but I didn't know what was happening. I was strung out."

Genesis House,[3] not far from the shelter, is a residence for women whose lives have been compromised by a potent combination of physical and mental abuse (often domestic), alcohol

and drugs, and the ongoing effects of cheap prostitution undertaken to feed a drug habit and maintain a pimp. Brenda's story
was the story of the women of Genesis House, a story to provoke
anger in those familiar with it, and shame at the knowledge of
what people can do to one another.

Brenda continues, her words powerful and disturbing: "I got
abused, and raped. I got my nose broken, got cut, and one time
got hit on the back of the head with a crowbar. I don't remember,
but he wanted me to give him some oral sex and I refused. When
I went to get out of the car, he grabbed me round my neck, and I
came out of my shirt—and that's the last thing I remember. I woke
up in hospital with a gash in the back of my head.

"Every day I woke up, I had to have it: the cocaine. It's the
price you pay. You take a chance. I went through a lot of weird
men. Weird men...They want you to do this, and that. It's kinda
difficult to talk about now. My attitude to men now: I will *never*
be with a man again. Because I've been abused so many times.
Men are not all bad...but I will *never* sleep with a man again. I
never enjoyed the sex with the 'tricks.' Twenty-five to thirty dollars a whop, sometimes more, and ten times a day, just for the
money to get cocaine. As for HIV, I always used protection, but I
got tested every six months. I just got tested two weeks ago. I'm
clean. The last sexual encounter was four, five months ago. It will
never happen again. I got a girlfriend now. I can't really explain
how you switch, but I've changed to being with a woman now.
It's comfortable. And it's much safer."

Brenda has finished describing the dark night, the depths, the
past. She has become quite positive over the past few months, and
senses real rehabilitation and recovery. That's what she wants
to talk about now.

"Right now, two of my kids are on the South Side, staying
with my girlfriend. My daughter is fifteen, and my son is seventeen. They won't have anything to do with me. They choose to
stay there. I guess they figure that now I've got a girlfriend [Darla,
her partner]...and they don't like that. I don't know. It's been two

months since me and her been together. But one day they are going to come to me. I just got to leave it in the Lord's hands. I know they're OK. I take them money when I can. A couple hundred dollars a month. I try to do day labor as much as I can. As long as they stay in school, I'm happy.

"I've tried being on my own, but I get very depressed. I cried a lot. But I get on well with Darla. When I'm with her, we talk about everything. The sex we have is OK. It's great, as a matter of fact! Right now we sit and talk about our kids. I got a son, Sergio, who doesn't even know his mother. He's ten, and they took him from me when he was five weeks old." As she shows her photograph of the little baby, she is evidently both proud, yet embarrassed, at how her life spiraled out of control. "He was addicted to cocaine when he was born. The last time I saw him, he was two. All I know is that he's in Harvey, Illinois. They won't tell me anything else. He has been adopted by his foster parents. I just would like to see him. I know I'm not going to get him back. The older one is in Indiana, with his father. We broke up in 1989 or 1990, because the state took my kids away from me. The other two kids are with Darla, but she is doing drugs now, and I don't choose to be around her. But my daughter and son choose to stay with her."

Brenda is now attributing free choice to her children, though it may be inertia, or inability on their part to choose much of anything. A pall of inevitability and fate hangs over Brenda: her family is virtually nonexistent (outside of her heart or memory); each of its members (former husband, current companion, grown children and more dependent children, herself) is in an unenviable situation with relatively bleak prospects.

This is a story rarely told and more rarely understood. It is the story of a woman whose life constantly takes her by surprise in ways that she simply cannot cope with; a woman whose early existence is so unstable that she has no realistic foundation on which to build a life; a woman whose experience with men is so identified with an experience of violence and abuse that she feels impelled to find community and companionship with another woman; a woman who gives up her child for adoption, fades from view, and is therefore assumed to have heartlessly abandoned her child. Every such story is so convoluted, so wrenchingly hard to hear, so impossible to make right—but here the protagonist is right before me and the story is no fabrication or composite of several different lives.

This is a true "inner story," and it helps to explain some general features of fostering, homelessness, and abuse. What strikes so forcefully, through Brenda's and others' stories, is just how little most people really understand (we may *know about,* but we do not really *know*) many social realities. There are thousands and thousands of Brendas, each with a story, and many still living with hope. If more people better understand the human face of homelessness, perhaps more appropriate ways would be found, to show real sympathy and meet the challenge of Jesus who will separate the sheep from the goats (see Matthew 25). Brenda, meanwhile, shifts focus and looks forward once again, thinking positively.

"I hope in a year from now[4] to have a good-paying job; an apartment, maybe a car. I hope that real soon my kids will want to come and live with me. Of all these, a job and an apartment are my biggest hopes. I go to day labor, but the job I was on last month is finished. I was working in a factory putting metal through holes. I'll go up again today, after I've finished here. I'll see if they have any work. I can earn about $40 in a day. I can get about $250 a week if I work the whole week. I'm not supposed to, because I am getting disability [SSI], but I'm just trying to get off the street.[5] They are already taking money out of my SSI because I worked last year. They take $46.50 out of my check: I don't get the whole $494. I get about $390 to live off of. Darla is working too, but she's sending money to her father to take care of her kids too.[6]

"There was a good [church] service yesterday, near the shelter I went to last night. I don't usually move from shelter to shelter, but REST has this lottery thing,[7] and I have to have some sleep. I don't want to be sleeping on the train to work. I want to ask God to get my kids back; to have a normal life; for me not to be on the streets. I feel a lot of other women give up. I feel that just because you're homeless doesn't mean you have to look or act like you're homeless. Today, a lot of people ask me, 'How did you become homeless?' I say, 'By using drugs and alcohol. That takes everything away from you.' But God tells me in my heart to keep going: 'Don't make yourself look like you're homeless.' So I try not to."

To listen to Brenda is to be impressed and edified. Her strength is unimaginable, as is her capacity to introspect, to acknowledge sin, to repent and to trust: "I do feel close to God. Right now. I'm doing a lot better now than I have in years. Only problem is... the shelter thing: you're not guaranteed to get in. I'm trying to get a case manager, and to work days to get money to get me a place. I have about two hundred dollars saved up, and I opened a savings account so that I wouldn't lose it or be tempted to spend it. The SSI money I get is because of psychological problems. I've been in and out of psycho hospitals. Last year, I was in almost the whole year. See, I hear voices a lot; voices telling me to hurt myself or hurt people. I can't figure out who they are. I hear them, but I don't know. It's like a bunch of people all at once. I don't know if it's God or the Devil. I don't know who it is. They tell me to hurt myself. I tried it before. Pills. I'm still seeing a psychiatrist now."

This is the very first indication (apart from her idiosyncratic "choosing") that Brenda is not stone-cold rational. But it's not surprising, given her early traumas, addictions, multiple complicated pregnancies-and-adoptions, and the violent abuse she has suffered. It is simply one more burden she must carry, virtually alone. The marvel is that she is able to move forward at all. Sisyphus comes to mind: the mythical Greek who was banished and condemned to roll a heavy stone to the top of a hill—only to have it roll all the way down when it was just short of the top.

"I would have an apartment by now, but I take money over

for my kids, to my girlfriend's. I gave her permission to try to get a LINK card [equivalent to food stamps] for my kids, if they want to stay with her. Then hopefully I will be able to take my check and get a place. My girlfriend [not her partner, Darla, but another woman friend] called the other day to say they are going to give the kids something [food stamps or card], so I'm grateful for that. Hopefully, by next month I'll have a studio apartment. I tell myself one day I'll have that and be like ['respectable people']. I don't get angry at them; I get angry at myself. Some people look at me like, 'you don't look like you are homeless,' because sometimes I don't have cigarettes and I stop someone on the street. I say, 'Well, Ma'am, I'm homeless,' and they say, 'you don't look like no homeless.' Now often I don't ask for cigarettes. I just do without. I don't like to get turned down when I ask. Most people are good: some are rude."

Does she truly think things are looking up for her? She says she does. "About six months ago I just got very tired of using drugs and alcohol. That's what took my life away from me, took my kids away. I think it drove my father to pass away. People keep telling me not to think I drove my father to his death. He died worrying about me…and drinking a lot. And he was diabetic on top of that. And he had cirrhosis of the liver. He was fifty-one." Is she serious or just very naive: does she really think he died of a broken heart…?

"I first started [rehabilitation] ten years ago when they took my kids away. I went into drug rehab. But I relapsed. About seven times. So, six months ago, I was just tired of seeing the lifestyle I'm living on the streets. And that [shelter] lottery thing really makes you wake up. It's kinda hard when your number don't get pulled and you don't know where you goin' to sleep that night. Being on the street, and a woman, is not good because you got a lot of weird men out there. I try to stay happy during the day, but I start getting depressed at night when it's time to go and stand in line [outside the shelter]. I can tell when there's going to be more than forty women, going to be too many, because if the line gets past the end of that alley, there's too many. So I like to help you [Tony][8] in the kitchen because that's a guarantee of a bed."

Does she feel ashamed? That, it turns out, is a question with far-reaching effects. "I don't feel ashamed, no. At one time, yes. I just have to keep faith with the Lord. I talk to a lot of ladies coming to the shelter, and I try to give them encouragement and advice. REST is a good program. I tell them to go through the program [systematically]. That helps really get you off of the streets. When I first came down here in 1990 I was in the program, and they gave me housing then. They get you a case manager and put you in the Northmere.[9] But I choose not to go that route again. I'm afraid, Tony, to stay by myself. I need someone to be with. It helps me to stay clean. But I'll never go with a man again. So, I have Darla. She has a difficult life, too. We lean on each other. She has two kids."

Then she says that Darla is just dying to talk with me...Darla will indeed talk, next. She will tell me about her life, and her life with Brenda. In fact, Darla will tell me more than even Brenda knows.

5

DARLA

The hour arrives, and so does Darla. Rather tense, and clutching the tape recorder, she begins to talk about her childhood.

"My name is Darla Danielle Jenkins. I was born here. I had a very good childhood. I was with both my parents for most of my life, but every year it seemed like we moved. My mother didn't like some locations. My father worked for the city. I have one brother. I did my first year of college. When I was eight years old…My parents argued a lot. My father was abusive. He hit her a lot. He was on drink and drugs. He did mental more than physical damage. She packed up, and we left with my brother a couple of times. One time she even moved all the furniture out. But we always moved back. She would go to her best friend's. She didn't have no brothers and sisters. My father did. I know them, but I don't associate with them. Because my mother…"

Twice already, Darla remembered something very painful. She quickly changes the subject. "My [paternal] grandmother passed away when I was eleven. They thought [my father] controlled all her money and stuff, which he did. But he used that money for the funeral. My mother had to take out a loan for her being cremated. They thought he took all the money for his personal use, but he didn't. He used it to have a funeral. Nobody else contributed."

Darla is not too clear, very self-conscious, and still trying to settle. When she focuses, it is upon her father. "My father is a control freak. I think the drugs played a big part, because any drug is mind altering. But when he got clean for about three years, he was going to meetings: he was even chairing meetings. My mother seemed a lot happier then, but he was still abusing her. Just little things. He liked to be waited on, hand and foot. And she catered to that. So, when she passed away two years ago, I went through a big thing because he started treating me like he had treated her."

Her eyes are alive now. She is more articulate, and capable of very rational judgment and comment. She knows exactly what she thinks.

How did her mother die?

"It was from a cocaine overdose. She was not always on drugs. She started when she was about twenty-seven. I was about seven. She was forty-three when she died. I tripped out because by that time I had started doing drugs... I was seeing myself becoming *him*." Not *her*.

Darla's life went seriously downhill at this time. No wonder. "Yeah. I don't know if they were breaking up, but the family were kinda separating. Me and my dad were not communicating. My mother and me were always together. She took me shopping. We did a lot of girl things together. But my dad was in his own little world. He started selling drugs. He was trying to teach me how to count drug money. He had thousands of dollars on the table and was telling me to count it. If I didn't, I would get my ass whipped."

This woman's story is mesmerizing. She is young and evidently a quick learner, (worldly) wise beyond her years. Having described her young life (the eight-year-old daughter of two cocaine addicts—one a seller, the other already dead—witness to violence between her parents and subject to physical abuse by her father), she now fills in some local detail: "My brother has cerebral palsy. He's not aware of what's going on. My dad looks after him. I'm twenty-four; he's twenty-two. My dad said if I didn't get good grades I was going to get ass-whipped. My father's a big man. He's too big to be hitting on anybody. He was a big time dope dealer. He made a lot of money. My mother didn't have to work, but she wanted to get away from him. That was her way of getting out of the house. At one time, he wanted her to stop working because he had too much money. Sometimes she would take her check and put it straight in the bank: she didn't have to cash it. He had money around all the time. He was working for the city—at a gas station."

Her father dominated her life. His behavior, and the inconsistencies between what he did and what he said, what he considered to apply to himself and what he meted out to others, left a profound mark on Darla's life and a very confusing legacy for her to deal with.

"He always told me whatever he was doing. Like, he would *show me*: 'here is a drug, and if someone ever brings it to you, tell them no!' He was always telling me to do the opposite of what he was doing. He'd say, 'you see I'm doin' something wrong. So you know to do the opposite!' That's how I was brought up. I thought, 'Well, damn! Daddy's telling me to don't do this, so don't do this.' At times I really despised him. I felt like hurting him because he was hurting my mother, but I knew it would be wrong for me to do that. There were times I physically wanted to hurt him, because of my anger. I'm looking at my mother and feeling what she's feeling and saying to myself, 'How can he do this to her?' What he was doing was so wrong, hitting her like that. She wouldn't talk to me then, or she would grab me and hold me and tell me I'm the only thing she loves. She'd say, 'I love you,' and tell me I'm the only thing she's living for."

What about her father? Did he tell her he loved her, and confuse things more?

"No...He told me a few times, but I never cuddled with him or talked to him. But he did take care of my brother..." Then she remembers that it really wasn't like that: "...or he paid someone to watch him if I wasn't there, if I was at school. My brother went to school, 'special school.' Most of the time when he got back from school I would be there to get him off the bus, and it would be just me and him."

Darla was her brother's keeper from an early age. Now she begins to reminisce about other formative influences in his life. "I was in Catholic school until second grade. That was where Mom wanted me to go. My mother went to church until my grandmother died. We all did. I went to Catholic church a few times, to visit; but not regularly. I went to the Baptist church. My grandmother went every Sunday and took me with her. In the summertime I would spend a few weeks with her at her house. So we would go regularly. I was her favorite. She spoiled me rotten. She fixed me breakfast and bought me things…I enjoyed going to church with her. I never knew my mother's mother: she died before I was born.

"I remember this lady, Madame Popsy. She was a psychic or something. I remember her telling my mother what I was seeing when I was still a kid. I had episodes of seeing things that just can't be physically explained. Like seeing a lady standing in a doorway telling me to tell my mother, 'It's OK; it's OK!' My brother was in the hospital with pneumonia then. I didn't know who the lady was. The doctors were telling my mother that my brother might possibly die. But this lady was telling me, 'It's OK, he's going to live.' Then a couple of weeks later he came out of hospital. That's one time. Sometimes I know when somebody around me is going to die. I see shadows. I still do. I don't know what it is. Shadows in the house. You can see the figure—no face, all black like a shadow. It's standing there. Every time somebody died in my family I saw the shadow. My mother did too. My uncle [father's brother] was in a car accident; my cousin; my father's best friend [a drug overdose]: all of them died. My mother told me the psychic lady said that the person in the doorway when my brother was ill was my mother's mother. I never knew her."

Darla is quite unassuming, rather matter of fact, but very serious. Later, I wonder whether she had had any premonitions of impending doom, but I never thought to ask her. I asked how she came to be at the shelter.

"Like I said, my mother passed away two years ago. I went through a lot of turmoil then. I was eight months pregnant. I was upset that she did not get to see her new grandchild. I was blaming myself, because I was with her when she died. I felt like God was punishing me. I felt I could have done more. Why would he take her away just when I needed her? This was my first child. I don't know anything about babies. I have no knowledge about what I'm supposed to do, how to feed, how to bathe [a baby]. My mother was trying to help me. She was giving me books, showing me what was going on inside my body. I didn't know any of that. I knew my dad wasn't going to do anything. All through my pregnancy he wasn't trying to help me in any way. All he said was, 'Where's the father?' He was no help. I felt closer to my mother because she was trying to explain it to me. I felt like, 'Why would God take her when I'm only a month away from having my baby?' But then they say God ain't goin' to give you more than what you can handle.

"My mother got on drugs through my dad. He was pushing her to it. She got hooked. She tried to stop, but only for two or three months. Then later, just like smoking, she quit for two years. But one day she got mad and started again. I know it got bad for her, because I was indulging with her. I had started smoking cocaine myself. People in the [housing] projects used to give it to me. For free. The baby is not a crack baby: I stopped just for those months. But the day after I had her I was out there doing it again. I waited until I had my baby. She was with me. It was in the building. I didn't even have to go anywhere. They brung it to me." It's easy to visualize Darla, a baby on one arm, smoking crack, and nursing the baby too. What about the baby's father?

"He was in the penitentiary. He was more like a fling: he was never concerned about the baby. The baby is with my dad. Now I have two girls. My father is looking after my brother and my two girls. The father of the second one is out here somewhere [in

Chicago]. I guess he's doing fine, but he won't come to me. He stopped me a couple of weeks ago to ask how his daughter is doing. He knows I'm in a relationship with Brenda now. I told him he could find out by visiting her at my father's. But he was never there, even when she was born. He don't even know what she looks like. She looks just like him. But he don't want to go.

"That was just a one-night stand. I must be honest. It was. We were consenting to this one-night stand. It wasn't a relationship. We had never indulged in any type of kissing or whatever. It was just straight sex. And that was it; I ended up pregnant. I never took precautions. I never slept with men that often.

"The kids are two and one. My father said that if I felt I couldn't live with him, he will look after them till I get on my feet. And I can't. Not with him hitting me. I'm not going to do it. I'm imagining my daughters getting their asses whipped, but there ain't nothing I can do. I have nowhere to take them. I have no money for an apartment. What am I supposed to do?"

History repeats itself. Darla has been whipped and raised by an abusive father and an effectively absent mother. Now her children are with her own abuser, while *their* mother is effectively absent. And who is this father who appears to offer to raise a son with cerebral palsy and two granddaughters—while still a junkie himself—and yet has terrorized his own daughter? How are those under his care suffering now?

"My father is not working now. He gets a check. My mother's Social Security check goes to him now, because they were legally married, as well as all the money she saved up, or was in her bank account. He gets eighteen hundred dollars a month. My brother gets nine hundred dollars. But my father gets all that too. He looks after my brother, my children, and his girlfriend. It's not like he's alone, and I trust her. There's been times when she babysat for me and I paid her while I went out with my friends. I'd rather they were with him [and her] than with the state.

"After the baby, and after my mother died, we got some money from her stocks and bonds. She worked for Illinois Bell for twenty-five years. And so we [my father and the baby] moved. He went on a wild party. I was trying to pack up my mother's things and sell her clothes and look after the new baby. She was a small lady and I'm a big lady. I was giving away her clothes and keeping little things of hers to remember her. I kept a lot of sentimental things. The rest of the stuff I left there, stuff I couldn't find a home for, or things I didn't know what to do with. Then we all moved, because they were going to renovate the building."

Darla is talking but is now becoming dissociated and incoherent. She seems to have distributed her mother's effects with more concern than she shows her new baby! Did things improve? The baby's father was incarcerated and Darla's father was looking after her first child. What happened next?

"I was working here at a temporary employment agency, from when I was nineteen to twenty-three, including maternity leave. Then I got pregnant again. My father got upset. I thought about an abortion but then I thought: 'No, because it was meant for me to have another baby. It was meant. Else I wouldn't be pregnant.' My mother always told me she never wanted me to have an abortion. So I went by that, and I did, and I ended up having my second child. My girlfriend was babysitting for me while I went to work, so I had someone constantly around.

"I had to work, look after the babies, sleep, and work…and on the weekends me and my dad would end up arguing because he expected too much from my girlfriend. I almost thought he was jealous. Brenda was living with us, but I was often giving him money for her to stay there. She got her check, and she was getting her money out of her check. It wasn't like she was trying to live there rent-free and eating up all our food. He tried to come to her sexually, and I got upset. I couldn't understand that, because he knew, from the very beginning, that we were intimate with each other. He had done it before, too, to past girlfriends I had. But they broke up with me and ran away because they were afraid of him. But she wasn't. She just told me, flat out, 'I'm not afraid of your father, but he's trying to have sex with me.' I asked my father why, when he knew we were together, and he said: 'Well, I don't have no name on it. Do you?' "

Will she talk about her girlfriends? "The first time, I was fifteen. I had a boyfriend first. But I prefer to be with women. Always. I been through some shit with men." Here is a very clear and simple statement about sex, sexuality, sexual preference, and sexual orientation: Darla is honest and worth listening to. "But it ain't just because I been treated badly. I have better relationships with women, whether friendship-wise or whatever: any kind of relationship. I can relate to women better. Think about it: if I know what I like, then I know more what she likes than I would know what you like."

Suddenly the dam bursts: "I been raped." Now she breaks down, sobs, and then apologizes to me. "I was nine. It went on a couple of weeks. He told me that if I told anyone he was going to kill my parents. And I didn't want to tell my mother because I was so scared that if I told her he would kill them. So I kept it inside. I waited until I was sixteen before I told my mother. She just kept looking at me like, 'Why didn't you tell me?' I told her because I was afraid and he was a friend of the family. Him and my father were real close. He knew my father was away during the day. It was near the house, by the bushes in the courtyard. One day my father asked him to watch me. It happened again. This time it was in the house. First time it was in the hallway. This lady was coming and I tried to scream so bad, but he put a sock in my mouth and I couldn't scream. The lady couldn't hear me. I was looking at this lady walking, but she couldn't hear me. I didn't know what to do and I tried to kick and fight and it didn't work. He just put his fingers in me, and stuff. The second time he made me give him oral sex."

As Darla talks, she reveals a glimpse of a world where a nine-year-old child is molested and brutalized by her father's "trusted" friend. Alien to me, it is the only world she has known.

"I was nine. I knew what he was doing he shouldn't have been doing to me. My mother always said, 'If someone touches you down there, you come and tell somebody.' But when he told me he was going to kill my parents, I couldn't say nothing. After that, I looked at men kinda different, like they were all going to hurt me. I did have one good relationship with a man that lasted for two years, when I was sixteen. I liked our friendship more than anything else. Sexually, I couldn't feel myself being there. It was like I was having sex with him but thinking of someone else—this girl I had a crush on. When I'm with a woman, it's much more relaxed."

Here is concrete reality: sex-abuse and its deep effects. The Church needs to understand it. No one can have compassion or empathy without a willingness to respect the experience of actual people. The nature/nurture issue is by no means clear: but early experience that alienates people from "the other" (whether sexual, parental, or peer) through a kind of "imprinting" *against* them, indicates more than an "objective disorder." Darla's father is a bully, addict, pervert, and procurer. No wonder she is "disordered." "Society" or "the Church" is sometimes a bigger part of the problem than of the solution.

The air is tense and Darla is very fragile. She needs to change the subject. The shelter is what brought Darla to this interview: how did she become homeless?

"Oh! Me and my daddy got into a big argument. He was high and intoxicated, and he hit me. And I felt: 'I'm a grown woman. I'm twenty-one. I'm not six anymore. If we can't sit down and talk, then I shouldn't be around. Something's very wrong. Anyway, I left my father. I didn't take anything except the clothes on my back. I didn't have any money. I went to my friend's house. I was sitting around (you don't want to wear out your welcome). So I bummed a transfer and came up here, and ran into my best friend who I hadn't seen in seven months. I left the kids with my father! [She seemed indignant that I should ask.] I wanted to take them with me, but I didn't know what to do. I insisted that I should leave them with him. If I took them, then he would just make it harder for me to get out the door. He didn't try to get me back.

"So my friend took me around Uptown, and I met these girls, Doris and Toni, and they were sleeping in the park during the summer. I decided I was going to sleep in the park, too. Never in my life had I done that. I was nervous, scared, angry—a lot of emotions. I was afraid someone would come up on me. I said, 'How can you sleep here, knowing that there's people?' After a while, I got used to it. They were kind to me. They showed me how to find all the places to eat, and the free bathrooms. They took me around. To the Jesus People—they give out blankets. I got about four or five blankets; that's how I started. Then I went to Sarah's Circle. I could do chores to get clothes and jewelry and all kinds of stuff, and I said, 'Hey! You can live out on the street!' Everything's in one area, within walking distance. But then I lost my job, because I wasn't sleeping right. Most of the time I was up during the night, because I was afraid someone was going to come and attack me. Anything. I was doing drugs. People I didn't know gave them to me. If you're nice to people, they'll come and offer you anything you want. Alcohol. Cocaine. Anything. There were a lot of Mexicans. I didn't do prostitution though. I never did that.

"Then I met Brenda. She was on and off at the shelter. I had seen her around. I didn't think she was gay, but I had a crush on her. When she approached me, it kinda freaked me out. I said, 'Why me? All these people out here.' But we got to know each other. She wanted me to stop harming myself; she was my inspiration. I actually stopped doing drugs. I'm clean now. We are keeping each other clean. She talked me into going to the shelter. I thought, 'Oh my God!' It was very different: something I had never experienced. Everybody's always afraid of new things..., like stepping behind a door. You don't know what you'll find there.

"That was still in July or the beginning of August. There were times I got turned away from the shelter, and I still had to sleep in the park. I got a counselor. I needed an ID, a SS card, and a birth certificate. They were all at my dad's house, and I didn't want to go back. I wanted to see my kids. I haven't seen them since I left—six months. My father does not have a phone, so I haven't talked to him and I don't know about my kids. I know they're not with the state. My friend said they were still with my father. Brenda says she will take me to see them next week. Both their birthdays are coming up—my father and Darneesa. Tylor is my other baby. My father thought of that name: he's from Tylor, Texas."

Darla has a real capacity for reflexiveness. She can step back, make a judgment, and act. Where does it come from? She says: "Well, I've had counselors and so on, since I was fourteen. For depression and things. I was institutionalized for two months. The second time for three months. Then only for a couple weeks. I went back when I was nineteen. They just said I suffered from depression. I took Prozac and Fluoristan. My mother had me taken off Prozac because she said it was making me more depressed. After that, I got on something else."

But it's not just medication; it's dedication. What keeps her going, apart from Brenda, her inspiration? "Next year, I'd like to be in an apartment, with my kids, and with Brenda. That's where I want to be. And it's realistic. But first I have to get me another job. I did have one, for three weeks, but my supervisor is prejudiced and I lost it. I'm not prejudiced. I can get along with everyone. Right now, I'm looking for a job. Brenda's not ready to work yet. She's had job opportunities: people keep calling her to go back to her old job. But she don't want to do it. Parts of her want to work and parts of her don't. But the more she sees me working, the more she might. Right now she's not going to do anything, but I'm going to find a job."

Darla senses that her determination can be both the catalyst for Brenda's and the basis on which to build the future. But who could know the future?

Will Darla talk more about herself? She will, and quite spontaneously now: "I don't think of myself as homeless: this is only temporary. I don't think people see me as homeless, 'cause I don't dress like homeless. When I was growing up, people that were homeless dressed the same way. I see that differently now, because a lot of homeless people don't dress any different from other people. There's always enough clothes at Sarah's Circle. They got my size. They got everybody's size. They give away socks and hats and gloves and everything. I got a locker. I keep most of my clothes in there. The rest I carry around with me: my clean clothes and my night clothes. And the clothes I have on, I take off, fold them up, and put in a dirty-clothes bag. We can wash our clothes at Sarah's.

"Sometimes I ask for a quarter, if I'm short or need to eat. I usually pick people I think will be kind. They may say, 'No, I don't have it right now' or 'I'm sorry.' Some are rude. They want to fight because you ask for a dime. It's like, 'Don't ask me for shit. Who are you?' So I walk away. I don't like confrontations. I've been volunteering, so for the past two months I've not been refused entry. By next month I don't see myself being here in this shelter."

Darla finishes on an upbeat note. She says she will talk with me again. She will, she does, but not for almost a year, and in circumstances neither of us could have visualized.

6

RANITA

Ranita is a security assistant at the women's shelter. I never knew she was a homeless person. But she has been homeless briefly, as well as "a hair away from homelessness." She is friendly and compassionate toward the women, and interested in me for two reasons: few men help at the women's shelter; and the women seem at ease with me (the newer women are quickly told that I am not a "problem"). But establishing relationships takes time. In the early days the women always called me "Tony"; these days (I am now older than most of them) everyone calls me "Father Tony."[1] That title acts as a "password" for women coming to the shelter for the first time: they find it acceptable.

Ranita knew the women were telling me their stories, and asked to be interviewed. She had a compelling story, and she certainly had a mind.

"I was born right here, in Chicago, on the kitchen table," she begins, without preamble. "My mom raised me and my sister and my brother. My dad was around, but he and my mother were separated. I really didn't appreciate either of them then the way I do now. My parents are both deceased. I feel kinda lost without them because I never got the chance to say I love them. I graduated from high school and did two years of college. I met my husband there, and we got married. That was in North Carolina.

I majored in special education, but due to financial problems I had to leave. So I came home and started working various jobs: construction, typing, office. I ended up doing security. It's been twelve years now. All over: downtown, suburbs, you name it. You need basically to know section 38 [penal code]. You carry a weapon. You protect others, property, and safety."

Ranita is off duty when she speaks to me: she has one hand on the tape recorder and the other around a cup of coffee. No gun. Coffee and a tape recorder I can handle, but not guns. Ranita seems entirely at ease. She is a certainly dedicated, but it is difficult to imagine her in a "crouch and fire" position.

She begins by saying that someone she knew recommended her for the security position. "I got the job in June [over eighteen months previously]. This was my first experience of a shelter, very different from security for buildings or offices. The opportunities here for the women are not great.[2] I was never grossed out by what I encountered here, but my question was always, 'Why? Why are these women here?' I was a hair away from being homeless myself then, and I now live in an SRO, the Harold Washington. I have tried to steer the ladies toward housing. Basically I'm a sounding board for them. They need someone to talk to—another female—who will listen. Some of them don't look like they belong in a shelter. Most just don't like the responsibility of paying the rent or being alone. They are alone because of family situations or financial or health reasons. They told me different stories."

What Ranita says is true, but it's more of an "outer" than an "inner" story: her actual experience of homelessness was very brief, and she has not been compelled to find a shelter bed. Every woman's inner story is different, unique to herself. Ranita is talking *generalizations*. Only when the women speak about themselves and tell their own stories do they become convincingly personal and *particular*. Ranita is interesting, but the first-person stories are much more urgent and ring more true. Her observations underline the fact that nothing can adequately replace the "inner story" of homelessness, or the "inner history" of a homeless woman. What are Ranita's thoughts on homelessness, mental illness, and abuse?

"The addictions are first, then the mental illness, then the abuse, in my eyes. The biggest problem is the drugs. But there are also mentally sick people who don't want to be institutionalized again[3] but are afraid to live alone because they can't look after themselves. The women are lonely and they look for others, men, to hold them or comfort them. The guys tend to take advantage. I knew a lady who lived in a crawlspace [under a house]. She liked her space, her freedom. I said, 'But you don't need to live like this.' She said, 'I don't want my own apartment, a controlled environment.' I think she was suffering from mental illness."

Ranita has interpretations of everything. She gathers scattered facts and fashions in a rather whimsical way. How has she succeeded in avoiding homelessness?

"I was working at the racetrack. My addiction was marijuana. I came up positive at a random testing and lost my job. I had to do classes, and I met someone called Terry, and he put me on to SROs. I wish I could find him to thank him! I had lost my job and could not pay the rent. Once my lease was up I had to move in with my sister. I was giving her four hundred dollars a month, and she was spending it on drugs, but I didn't know that. She ended up putting me out. I was lost. Another friend of mine let me in. Then I applied for an SRO. Within two weeks I got in.

"So it was my stepsister who gave me the initial opening. The blood sister and I are not close: she is pretty well-off, but there's a jealousy there. I've never understood why we couldn't get along. But before I would ever move into her house I would go to a shelter, because we would be bickering and fighting…This goes all the way back to childhood. I was the favorite. I'm not sure what that means. I asked her. I cried. But it bothers me."

Something is buried deep here, and Ranita does not want to elaborate: something about a stepsister not accounted for, and a sister with whom her relationship has never been strong, and a brother who does not enter the picture. But she is adamant that she would rather be on the street than ask for hospitality from her sister.

"The family makes such a big difference [in any life]. If you have a parent or a sibling, you might at least have a place to go. My parents did tell me they loved me. Often. I was seventeen when my mom died, and in my thirties when my dad passed." Ranita is forty-six now.

How was her marriage? "It was great! He was brother, sister, father to me: everything in the world. But I couldn't give him a kid. I felt very inadequate—*he* didn't make me feel that way. I told him he needed children and that his mother needed grand-children. It just wasn't my time, or I couldn't hold him…" Her desolation is palpable, recalling those biblical women who were barren and so deeply yearned for a child. But then I realize I have misunderstood: Ranita was not infertile! She continues: "I really believe that it was the hospital that killed my baby. They told me I was Rhesus negative and that they were taking the fluid out of the sac so that the baby wouldn't be jaundiced. But every time I visited the hospital they took the fluid, so the baby had no fluid! It was a full-term boy, and he died inside me. Stillborn. I tried five times with my husband, and then I gave up. I walked away, and I didn't cry. I was drinking and smoking marijuana. I was in my early twenties, and it was because I couldn't have kids. I started going to bars. He followed me, but I kept on pushing him away. So I went back to my parents. He divorced me on grounds of desertion. We still have contact. We are still good friends. He's married with five children. I talk to his mom. He's a firefighter in Evanston. And he has his own construction business."

Ranita can sound glib then suddenly become a philosopher. She must have found it very difficult to realize that she was not entirely in charge of her own fate. Then she seems to change the subject. "I'm bisexual. I wanted to venture out and see another part of the world: to explore, to open up. I have sexual attrac-tions to women. I knew that very early, very far back. I was young: eight or nine. I had bad experiences, too. I was sheltered, but wild too. My parents kept control of me. My dad said if I kissed a boy I would get pregnant. That was all the sex education I got.

"If I had a relationship with a woman now, that would be security for me. We are women. We think alike. We know what each other needs, and so on. We would protect each other, like, 'I won't let anyone hurt you and you won't let anyone hurt me.' Actually, I would prefer to be secure, and to be with a partner, somewhere else. That, to me, would be living. I'd have a real life. As it is, I work, and I come home. But the Harold Washington is my security."

"My dad didn't have a clue how to look after kids. I was seventeen [when I had a baby]. My mom told me everything, nice— but he [her father] made it threatening. Before she died my mom said, 'Whatever you do, please graduate out of high school. And whatever you do, please be a lady.' I'll never forget that. She was under the influence of alcohol, but I'll never forget. I still hear that today."

Ranita seems never to have felt good about herself. She says she could not please her husband, or her father, or even her sister; and her mother died when Ranita was only seventeen. Even now, thirty years later, Ranita is always comparing herself unfavorably with others—though she tells herself that she is just as good as they are. She talks about this.

"In my adulthood I had one bad, abusive relationship. I got out of it in time. I spoiled him rotten. I was forty-four, just two years ago. But if I wasn't home at a certain time he would take a swing at me. The first time, he was drunk, but not the second. So I said, 'Oh no! I'm not going to deal with this!' I was trying to have a heterosexual relationship, deliberately. I think I wanted someone in my life permanently. I'm still trying to find out who I am. I don't have a relationship with a woman at present, and I don't want one. *I'm still trying to love myself.* That goes way back. I'm afraid to look inside myself. One day I'm going to find out. I just don't know when."

Ranita identifies two social facts: precarious living conditions, and a precarious personal and social or psychosexual identity. One alone produces challenging and frightful experiences: both together must make life nightmarish. Many people with minimal family support and incomplete education, so easily and quickly fall into a social and religious void. Unless the Church—and particularly its professional ministers—learns more about it, and then finds ways to encounter such persons, we stand accused of laying intolerable burdens upon others, burdens we are unwilling and probably unable to carry ourselves. Ranita articulates the cry of the poor, the cry we say our God hears, the cry all godly persons should become more attuned to.

"I stay focused. I know I can be centered. Childhood, being obese, being not pretty—these are the problems. I was in grade school. I was inside, and also outside. My sister mainly [was the opposition or the competition]. If you're not pretty, and obese, who wants you? During my marriage, that was fine. He loved me for who I was. My personality was fine. He tried to reassure me, to have us adopt a baby. But I wanted to give him a child from me. And I didn't accept the love he offered. I think I could accept it now. I know he still loves me. He told me that. *But I haven't learned to love myself yet.* I would like to know what my problem is, deep down inside. Maybe I'm suppressing something. *I really, really want to know.*

"The treatment I get from my coworkers and my boss makes me feel that something's wrong with me, because I'm not getting the same treatment as them. I try to give 110 percent, but my boss has made five people supervisor since I came. Why can't I be supervisor? One answer I got was, 'I didn't hire you. [Another person] hired you [so he would be responsible for promoting you].' I get blown off every time. A supervisor has more authority, like Teresa, Shawn, or Vicki. I'd like to be a supervisor, if I could get another twenty-five cents raise. But no one asks me for advice or suggestions. To me, I have supervisor qualities. I could do things [my boss] would be proud of. I go home and cry, and ask God to help me.

"I get on very well with the women. A lot of them respond to me. But some of my coworkers want to get rid of me. They seem jealous of me. I don't understand it. A lot of the ladies respond well to me, but the staff don't like that. One of the supervisors made it very clear to me: 'You are not the supervisor. The ladies will not do what you say. I am the one to do that.' And it hurt me terribly. The Polish lady kissed me the other day. She said, 'You are so good!' I really feel the warmth from a lot of them. There's nothing much I can do to help them but just be there. One of the supervisors asked me, 'What am I doing wrong?' I told her that she kept reminding the ladies that they are in a shelter: they don't want to be reminded of that."

How does Ranita come to be sitting in this little room in Chicago, talking with me? How did I come to be listening to this excellent diagnostician who just wanted to be loved, and who was quite aware of the circumstances that made that so unlikely? How did she become so articulate, giving birth to thoughts she didn't know she could deliver, and perhaps even beginning to love herself a little more in the process? Mystery is the fabric of life.

Ranita's plight is indeed sad. She is forever willing, competent, eager to please, and—a rarer quality—patient and considerate with the women. Other staff members give rather odd looks but little positive response when asked whether Ranita will make the grade. She truly does her best and is truly gifted and graced in some areas—yet seems to get nowhere in terms of upward mobility. It is very sad to see such a good woman overlooked and bypassed in this way. But Ranita is not done, and she picks up the conversation again.

"[I'm most proud of] staying at one job for any length of time. I've been with REST five years. I've never been at any other job for more than a year. I was the black sheep of the family. This is like I'm saying to my dad, 'See, I did it! I can do it!' I was the crazy one; I didn't have all the marbles; I did some stupid things. But everyone else—Mom, Dad, brother, sister—were slow learners,

EMH students.[4] I finished my school! I was very rebellious, very angry against authority, especially when my mom died. And my dad was very, very strict with me. He would kick my butt for any little thing, anything that wasn't to his satisfaction. He would get a belt to me. He was a Pullman porter for Amtrak. I was the middle child: the middle child, you get your ass kicked. I got locked out and ran away from home once. He said, 'You're not here to party.' I went to a party and got home at around 11:30 PM. He wanted me home by 10:30 PM. I was around seventeen. He just locked me out."

That was not the last straw, but it might have been the last incentive. She says, "I went straight to college then, and he paid for it! I'm sorry I didn't go into the military. I tried to go at the age of thirty-four."

Back to the subject of the women and homelessness, Ranita reveals some more of herself: "I'm not going to say they don't care, because a lot of them do care. But most [of those who don't care] are drug addicts: the ones that smoke up their money. Just about all of them at the shelter are addicts [something that certainly escaped my notice, after twenty years of close encounters].[5] Penny over there is an addict: the one with the blue jogging suit.[5] I don't know why, but I wanted to take her clothes and wash them for her. I want to have an emergency box somewhere for the women's needs. I would love to have socks, undies, or facecloths for them. But I can't do that because I'm not the program director. But I often want to say, 'Let me wash that for you.'"

Years ago, before budgets and paid supervisors, one of the volunteers would do the laundry during the night while everyone was sleeping. By morning, the women's clothes would be washed and dried and ready for wear. Some things can be done better on a small scale. Ranita continues, softening her previous remarks, or perhaps looking for approval: "Addicts are not necessarily mentally ill. They just have an addiction. But not many are doing much about it. Some are. I've seen some of them really trying. And some of them make it! It does my heart good to see them come by and say, 'See, I got my apartment!' Miracles do happen. But we had a couple who died and didn't make it."

As she remembers these things, some long-forgotten, I remind her that I will always take care of the burial of anyone who dies and for whom no arrangements have been made. She is very excited, and says, "I didn't know that!" She promises to keep the word on the streets. But she is reminiscing and philosophizing now.

"[People who become homeless are] victims of society, but also they bring it on themselves. One girl told me how her father used to beat her. Others are out there abusing [drugs, bodies], and they can't pay the rent. Some try to come for counseling, and it helps some. They know they can come and get a case worker if they want. But [other] people may steer them away. The streets steer them away. Suddenly they are distracted. They really have to want it: to want to get help and get off the streets. Like one girl. She's in the Northmere right now. I was with her last night, and she was so happy to be out of the shelter."

Finally, Ranita's hopes. She takes a deep breath and speaks with great passion. "I really wanted to move up in this company [the REST organization]. When I was hired, I was really given the impression that I could. But I'm still a security officer. I don't want to be a security officer the rest of my life! But 'they' don't seem to have confidence in me. I think I could make a real contribution, but...I can't understand it: why can't they just make up a new title for me? I don't have to be a supervisor. I am for the ladies 100 percent. I want to work for them. We have seven ladies from my shelter at the Harold Washington.[6] I don't want to live alone, but in the Harold I feel safe. You have to be announced, buzzed, in and out. No one can break in. Sometimes I don't want to come out of that building! I do want one bedroom, but I'm actually afraid to be by myself. I have been followed home.

"I think about counseling sometimes. But I can live with myself. I do have pride. I cook and I clean. But I do like to do for others—and then I forget myself. I'm really interested in the ladies and where they go. But we are not allowed to have any relationship with them. I'd like to invite them for a meal, but that's not allowed. Professional conduct. Two supervisors were fired for that. You can't do that. I've told the ladies, 'Sorry, you can't come up; I would lose my job.'"

The interview draws to an end, leaving the image of a very good woman who has managed without her unhelpful family, exorcized her drug demons, lived with her childlessness, paid the cost with her marriage, struggled with her sexuality, and survived. Yet she feels deep down that she is not respected, that she does not present well, and that she is not really going anywhere. Life is so precarious, yet people can survive with virtually no support system—and be truly altruistic. It will be interesting to hear her speak later, about fate, providence, destiny, and God.

7

LYNETTE

Every story is different, yet common threads connect the
human community. A structurally perfect family—good
education, the gift of beauty, and intelligence without a
trace of mental impairment—cannot guarantee happiness or success. This we know. But impaired family structure—lack of education, plainness of form, awkwardness of demeanor, modest intelligence or moderate mental impairment—are not inevitable in-
dicators of misery or failure. Sadly, people accustomed to good
health, success, and happiness may come to take these things for
granted, and even, at times, to claim credit: that is naive and shal-
low. More unconscionable would be the conclusion that both success and failure are entirely due to the dispositions of individuals.

As we absorb the inner history of homelessness, we can be
both horrified and edified, grateful for the light that illuminates
our pathways and sympathetic toward those whose lives seem
more clearly marked by long shadows. Complacency and condescension have no place in the Christian repertoire, but compassion and concern most certainly do.

The seventh of our symbolic twelve stories is as different as
each of the others, but common threads are becoming increasingly visible. Lynette's inner history offers us another opportunity
to listen and perhaps to hear and understand.

"I was born in Chicago and am almost thirty-seven. I have been homeless on and off for seven years. I was brought up in a very privileged household, even though I didn't have both parents: my mom was unable to take care of me and my sister and brother, so we went to our mother's mother when I was seven and my brother was a little baby. My parents were not married, and I did not really know my father. My grandparents forbade contact with him. I was brought up by my mother and her parents. I got ill when I was about eight—not long after I went to live with my grandmother. My mother was unable to pay the health insurance costs, and after we went to my grandmother's I didn't see my own mother much because she didn't visit. I remembered her only very slightly. But then, later, she became part of my life. A few years ago she broke her leg and was in rehab for eighteen months. I helped look after her. When I was young, she had an alcohol problem, and my grandparents were not tolerant of that. My father must have had a similar problem, otherwise he would not have been able to stay with my mother all those years. My grandfather died when I was twenty-five, about twelve years ago. My grandmother died last year. The building they lived in was sold, and my mother moved to Mississippi to live with her sister. She is fifty-eight now."

An intense, compressed story. So much for "a very privileged household"! Perhaps it will make more sense later. Lynette continues, slipping back and forth between childhood and adulthood in a stream-of-consciousness movement. "My happiest memories were the holidays. We always had family celebrations. Aunts and uncles on my mother's side. There was nobody on my father's side. I know where my brother and sister are. My brother was raised by his father's parents. He used to visit me. My brother and sister turned out fine. He is an evangelist. He still comes over. He is concerned. He wants to know when I'm going to move, and so on…She [her sister] is a sales person at Marshall Field's. I graduated from City College."

Why don't siblings look out for one another? What causes

family disintegration? But Lynette is off again, casually juxtaposing jobs and motherhood: "I've had jobs and children on and off. My problem started when I…I had DCFS (Department of Children and Family Services)[1] problems. My oldest daughter is sixteen now, but she was adopted at age seven by her father's mother. I'm always trying to prove myself a fit mother, and I've had a lot of drug problems: rehabilitation, homelessness, the court, problems with my case worker. You know how it is. But it's been coming out pretty good so far.

"My drug of choice was crack cocaine. I have seven children by two different fathers. One of them is dead now, or we would probably still be together. The oldest, Ladora, is in California from what I hear. The rest are here in Chicago: in foster care. I make it a point to get my visit, because I was not receiving them when I went into treatment several times. Four of them are in one place, and three in the other.[2] I'm lucky: some families get fractured, but they tried to keep all mine together. I see them every month."

Lynette is animated and enthusiastic: for her the glass still looks half full, while little more than dregs are visible to other eyes. Lynette is struggling with many demons: her past, the present, and even those that threaten to compromise her future. She fights them off, as she continues her story, looking for light, for encouragement. But what of the children's chances?

"I see them every month. I feel they are being cared for as properly as possible by the lady that has them. My case worker says I have made tremendous progress. The last time we spoke, she told me she wanted me to have my children back."

Hope springs eternal. Here is a woman with half a dozen dependent children, no adult male presence, one deceased and one departed father of her family, a foster parent of whom she says she approves (though her tone says something else), and a future grounded in her own shifting dreams. Yet she is here, talking, trying to make some choices and to move forward, and actually articulating her fragile hope. Is she a responsible person?

"Yes, I'm responsible. As long as I'm not using drugs. I have the utmost responsibility as long as...It was those drugs that interfered with, you know...my life. I don't know how my children are affected by drugs because my case worker has not done any background explaining how they feel. But I ask them questions, you know, about the things I did. But do they remember? They was very small at the time, so some of them don't."

Lynette is becoming increasingly vague and evasive, and distracted by her own memories. Despite her claim that she had a very privileged household, she was unquestionably taken away from her parents, brought up by a much older generation, and left with memories of both parents' abuse of alcohol. She may have been born with fetal alcohol syndrome. If so, history has already repeated itself; and given what she says about her own children (whose circumstances are certainly no better than her own were), it may well do so again. And what of the cocaine?

"None of my children are cocaine positive. None. They remember Mom. When we have a meeting together, they all come and hug and kiss me. 'Where you been, Mom,' Lanisha asks. She's nine, so she's in charge, right? She says she's glad I'm trying to get a place. When I'm leaving, she asks the same question as the boys: 'When are we leavin' here, Mom?' But things take time. I'm working on it. My case worker is working on it. Eventually things will work out. It will loosen up."

Lynette is completely out of touch with the reality that grounds other people. Perhaps it is her safety valve, but in no way can she be described as a responsible adult. She cannot separate herself and her children, in terms of status and role, the way a mother must. She seems to be at the developmental and emotional level of a not very alert or responsible child. She laughs when she tells me that Lanisha, at nine years of age, is in charge. She seems to think it's cute, and funny. Sadly, Lynette is mentally and emotionally unstable. Naming each of her seven children with the same initial as herself may not be certifiable behavior, but certainly indicates quirkiness. Yet there is an earnestness about her, a desire to convince and to find approval, and an apparent willingness to do whatever it takes to rehabilitate herself and regain custody of her children. It is a daunting, forlorn, and essentially futile task. Does Lynette think *anyone* is on her side or can help? She speaks of her sister.

"I guess she's at the point that...She took the position that if I was using drugs I really was not in the right frame of mind—which I wasn't. But I've noticed that she kinda supports me, because she was so very glad when she heard that I had heard from the children and she saw their pictures. She was happy, and glad I'd been through treatment. Yes, I think she supports me fully, now. She's really been trying to...; she's one of the main reasons why I did go to the treatment center. She told me: 'If you go into the treatment center and straighten yourself out, they will let you have your children. But you're going to have to show them. You have to change your life, otherwise they are not going to let you have your kids back.' She's right, I guess."

Lynette now knows that her siblings did not understand hard drugs. She acknowledges that she built her own habit secretly. "I supported my habit by stealing. I was jailed for shoplifting or scrapes. It began when I was at a party. I must have been about twenty-one, and it took me a year to build the habit to a hundred dollars a day, at least. I would steal from grocery stores and drug stores. I sold the stuff. I knew it was wrong, but when that stuff takes control of your life, you can't help it. You don't realize you are going down."

She talks about her habit, her pregnancies, and her children, maintaining (without much conviction) that she only did drugs when she was not pregnant. "I had a baby first. I started doing drugs after, long after, about a year after I had her. My mother's mother was looking after her. I tried to keep up with her, but unfortunately my family members thought she would be better somewhere else. Then I had no child for seven years. Then I had one. Then the father [of both children] died. That surviving child is nine now. Then there are five other children by a second man. I was getting pregnant every year. I *was* on drugs then. Life was really terrible. I didn't have any feelings at all. It didn't seem that I had any place [in the entire universe]. I was trying to find myself but getting lost in that place of drugs. I really don't know what happened to the kids. I'm hoping they understand. My grandmother was looking after most of them. Since the whole thing started, it's been really rough on me, but I stuck it out."

It almost sounds as if she is talking about a litter of puppies rather than a growing family; the "I'm hoping they understand" sounds too sad for words; and the focus upon herself at the expense of any real understanding of her children's plight is truly pathetic.

"The youngest, Latoya, is two now. She was in foster care from two weeks of age. I don't know what went on because I was not at the court proceedings. All of the children went into care at the same time—1997, 1998, something like that.[3] Their father was around, but I really didn't pay him much attention. He was trying to help me with the children. He was trying to watch them, buy clothes and shoes, take them to his house..."

Truly, the children are the first victims! But what about that man to whom she "didn't pay much attention" but who had fathered four of her children while she was addicted to drugs! Perhaps he only *thought* he was the father; perhaps she had *persuaded him* that he was. If so, one of them was smarter than appeared and the other dumber than imaginable. What were Lynette's thoughts? She was laughing as she started to speak.

"I really don't know why that was happening. The last time I went to Cook County Hospital, I asked to have my tubes tied, but they wouldn't, because they said I had had a stillborn baby and I might want another child. But when you go to these hospitals, there's such a backlog of people for tubal ligations, they don't want to see you unless you are in some kind of planned parenthood program. But I think it's wrong; they ain't the ones to help you to take care of your children, so they should tie your tubes. Me personally, I love my children. Don't get me wrong. But it's been very hard for me trying to take care of them and deal with different things and this and that, especially with the father of my first two dying. It was very hard."

Lynette speaks truth as she sees it, and no doubt the basic logic of those hospital officials is deeply flawed. Time and time again, as the women talk, they tell stories of people who were never deeply loved, never adequately affirmed—but nevertheless expected to take responsibility for their own children. They indicate the abundance of negative judgment but less than positive advice or assistance from "society"—and "The Church."[4] Does she feel victimized by society, by fate, or by God? She is quick to respond. "No. Oh no! No. The whole situation was my fault. The first four children are OK now; the last two are very young. I don't know if they have a grasp of the situation, as to what effect things are having. Lenisha (nine) knows what's happening, and I think she's holding up pretty well. But it's very hard for people to make it, especially children. It has been very hard for her, but she's doing very good. They take her to a counselor, and she's been seeing a psychiatrist. I think the boys may be going too. I'm not very sure."

Lynette shows no sign of grasping the chronic and unconscious traumas that affect children like her own. She seems to take literally their verbal assurances, on the rare occasions they are together. Unless they say they are suffering, they must be fine, she thinks. And off she goes again, on another track, moving away from the children and their needs and back to herself and her own.

"I have a psychiatrist, too. That helps a lot. My case worker asked me to see a counselor/psychiatrist. I can talk about whatever. Some things I wouldn't tell my case worker. There's privacy. But we talk about a lot of things. If I had not been receiving counseling, I don't think I'd be in the position I am today." God bless her!

"My psychiatrist helped me to figure out a whole lot of things about my life. That I have an addiction problem. That I was manic depressive. I get very low, depressive spells. I'm very easily agitated, moody, restless, over talkative. The medication has helped a lot. Since I was eleven or twelve I have been depressive. My doctor says it's a physical, chemical, imbalance. My grandmother would take me to the doctor, and he said it was ADD [attention deficit disease]. But recently my psychiatrist says it's more depressive. It may have had something to do with my parents and the situation at home. But there's not really mental illness running in my family, so I don't think my children...But there *is* instability, and it's occurring again, in my children's life."

Lynette is quite lucid now. Will she go back to the beginning of her experience of shelter living? She says she has been in the shelter only for three months or so, but that she has been living in other shelters for seven years.

"Lenisha was a baby. My sister put me out of my grandmother's house. I went to the police station and they took me to a shelter. I was there a year with my baby. At first I felt so out of place. I didn't know what to make of all these people. I didn't know what was happening. I was in kind of shock. I was treated nice. Sister Gerry was in charge. After a month they asked if I had a place and what did I want to do. They pulled a housing number and sent me to HUD [Housing and Urban Development]. Finally they got me an apartment. The father was with me. But in the winter I didn't have any heat. I was still using drugs. It was rough. Eventually I closed my apartment out. I was back in a shelter— for four months, waiting for housing. Then I went back to my grandmother's house, until they finally took Lenisha (five) and Lamar (three) into custody. Lavelle, my little boy, was the newborn. I named him after his nurse, so it's actually a girl's name! He's four now."

It seems extraordinary that most of the women seem not to be consumed by anger or bitterness. Is there something of a survivor instinct in these women that enables them to continue despite dreadful odds? Perhaps it's virtue.

"I have to put a positive spin on life. My psychiatrist reminds me of that. I'm not angry with anyone. No. I have never envied other people. I'm always preoccupied with what I'm trying to do. I won't say that life has been unfair. I've had a whole lot of blessings. Some things have not gone the way I would like. But I've never been [beaten up or raped]. I'm the type of person that, when anything happens, I'm outa there, you know! I'm not going to hang around. My sister used to get angry. [After Lenisha and Lamar were taken into custody] she got very angry with me. I don't know why. Probably because I was using [drugs]. Eventually my baby boy's father got himself together, and we put a down payment on an apartment. This was about four years ago. I never gave up. I was very determined that I was going to see my children. I felt that I just *had to make it*. I had them on my mind constantly. I didn't do anything special; I'm just their mother. But I did everything not only for me but for them too, to let them know that I do love and care for them.

"I stopped using last year. I wanted to, for one thing; [but] I got cocaine-related pneumonia. It was rough. That started a chain-reaction and I went to a treatment center. My sister was glad to hear it! I was there for two six-month programs. There was help, counseling, and we had some church: not forced, but optional. There were twenty mothers in PPWI [Post Partum Women and Infants], and about the same number of people in the second program.

"I'm trying to go on now. Every day is a meeting, AA, NA. I'm on public assistance. That's enough until I get Social Security. I don't know how I got to REST, but I do know I've been in almost every night [being lucky with the lottery]. I only 'lost' one night! I still go to outpatient [clinics] for rehab. I feel so much better. Life is definitely worth living. I have not felt this good forever. Before I started this medication I was in a different world, a different time period. I have no desire to go back to drugs. I don't even get the sensations. I have to look at my children, and at the big picture now. One of my cousins is helpful: she is always trying to encourage me. I do have ambition. I want to go back to school.

I want to be gone from the shelter in a month from now. If I'm on SS by then, *I will be gone.* It's time to get an apartment. On my own. No SRO. I'll continue with my counselor/psychiatrist. She's the reason I'm seeing my children now."

Lynette is a woman of great fortitude and admirable determination. Her story is enlightening and her resilience impressive. Her life has by no means been easy, but it is a life. Her last words, to herself and to me, were, "I've been lucky." Unbelievable! Lynette did not return to the shelter. Maybe her luck held. I never saw her again. But there's a lot of children out there, and a lot of struggle ahead.

8

LISA

We sit, as always, in a cramped room, Lisa with my small tape recorder in one hand and a cup of coffee in the other. The "deal" is always the same: for an hour of her time, each woman gets coffee, doughnuts, and five dollars. Anthropological training warns of the dangers of interviewee-bias—the possibility that people will say what they think we would like them to say. But doughnuts and dollars will hardly corrupt the women or their testimony.

Lisa sets off like a filly from a starting gate, eager and enthusiastic; but there is a darker side to her story, and soon it will slow her down and sap her strength. "My name is Lisa Coleman and I was born here in Chicago. My parents are both deceased. They were married and brought us up, five girls and four boys. I graduated from twelfth grade. We kids could have anything we wanted. When my mom and dad were alive, we wanted for nothing. My father owned a laundromat. We lived in the projects, at the Robert Taylor Homes. It was a happy childhood. And peaceful. Yes."

She stops, confused, or perhaps remembering something else or something different. What she says just doesn't sound right. No plausible sentence could contain both "Robert Taylor Homes" and "happy and peaceful." Perhaps she had some bad childhood memories. She certainly did, and some really bad stuff comes flooding back. But she starts off with a flat denial. "No. No bad memories at all. Everything was fine. Good school life. But the *neighborhood*...Oh! There's a lot of things I saw in the neighborhood. Like people getting killed. Yes. Going to school, they used to shoot. One building against another. Girls going to school, they used to shoot them. I ran across dead people; fell over them. I was thirteen the first time. They was shooting. I fell over this dead man. I got up and ran, back to the building, not to school."

Later she will talk about her deceased parents. They died just before that incident. What can life have been like then? How had she coped? She evidently has some deeply traumatic recollections, but she is talking more fluently now, though not more coherently, because she constantly moves back and forth in time and through space. What she says is compelling.

"The police were afraid to come to the projects. They didn't SERVE AND PROTECT us at all. The place was lawless. Controlled by gangbangers. My parents said, 'If they shoot, just run'— so I did. With my family, I always felt loved, but the neighborhood was another story.

"My parents died, nine months apart. I was thirteen. My mom died from bleeding ulcers. My father was murdered in his laundromat. It was shocking. I didn't know what death was until then. I was in the house. Somebody came up and said, 'Your father is hurt real bad.' He was dead. It was real bad. It was self-defense and they let the [shooter] go. My father was trying to shoot him, and the guy shot my father first. He was lying on his gun when they turned him over. I knew the guy. He was a friend of the family. I never did know why.

"My brothers and sisters had trouble. My oldest brother and sister got arrested for murder. They were gangbanging themselves. I'm thirty-three now, and she's three years older than me, but this was before my father died, about twenty years ago. Anyway, some of the other gangbangers tried to kill my brother (eighteen). He was in the gangs too. He had won a card game, and the others retaliated—another gang it was. My brother killed one of their members, but then all my brother's friends ran away. My sister (sixteen) came out of the apartment and shot the guy that was going to shoot my brother. Everybody had guns in the project. A week later my brother and sister were arrested and stayed locked up for two months. But my father was a (Free) Mason and he got them out. He's a 32-degree Mason.[1] The case was dropped."

This story makes complete sense. But the chronology seems wrong. If this murder happened when her sister was sixteen, then Lisa was about thirteen. But her father was still alive, and she said that the first dead person she actually encountered was when she was thirteen. Perhaps someone was shot in the projects, *and* her sister killed a second man, *and* her father was murdered, all in the same year, a few months apart. Or perhaps the body she fell over was in fact the person her sister killed. Either way there is wall-to-wall trauma here. It clearly marked Lisa's life.

"Everyone else in my family is in Mississippi now. They all have land. They got it from my mother's mother. I wouldn't want them to know about me right now. And I just can't stand Mississippi. There is real prejudice there. All my brothers and sisters were born there. But not me. So, they returned home. But they get called niggers and all that. Me, I got a very quick temper, so I know what would happen. My brothers and sisters contact me from time to time, but they don't know what I'm doing. As far as education is concerned, everyone got at least to ninth grade. One got to college. Two are married. The rest are with people [partners]. But I'm single. Never been married. No children. Never! I always say I'll have a child when I get married. I'm not ready to have a child yet, with the predicament I'm in."

Lisa seems quite reflexive and focused, in some ways; but fires smolder within. Her thoughts pour out in a stream of consciousness, compelling and confusing to me. She wants to talk, so she does; it is a struggle to hang on and follow her train of thought. It is a wild and fascinating ride.

"Drink has been my problem. Not drugs. Drink's a drug, ain't it? Anyhow, I ain't had a drink for two years now. I don't need

AA meetings. I once got drunk and blacked out. When I woke up I had a hangover and I didn't like that. I was alcoholic. I used to go to sleep drinking and wake up drinking. You gotta have the will power. I got it. From God. God goes all the way back, as far as I remember.

"I've had partners. None has ever been abusive to me. I look for people long-term, and one guy I was with for ten years. One night he left. I don't know what happened. Six months ago, when he left (I'd been laid off from telemarketing; I was bringing home eight hundred seventy dollars a week for two and a half years) I had no way to pay the rent. We had been paying it together. But when I got laid off he just got tired of paying. He left. I was homeless. I was evicted. I was homeless."

Such a fragile existence; such a small margin for error; so little between relative security and acute insecurity. But Lisa continues: "So I was sleeping in the park with all those [homeless] people. I'd never done that before. It was scary! I was afraid someone would come over from the lake, and get me, or hurt me, or kill me. Or that some crazy person might just come and start shooting up on everybody. I had never been homeless before, and I was not in a shelter. The weather was warm enough for sleeping outside. Everybody had a number to their tree. I was number nine. The people already out there made those decisions. You have to be part of the group. They welcomed me. But that's what made me feel scared: like, all of a sudden, why are they welcoming me?"

Humanity is naturally gregarious, and it is interesting, and impressive, to see how we organize and walk the line between hostility and hospitality. Lisa, acquainted with hostility yet looking for hospitality, is unnerved when it is offered: instinct suggests caution. But things turn out all right, though Lisa finds the people she is with to be less self-determined than she would like.

"There are men, women, and children, and they just lay out all day. They look after their trees and their things, otherwise someone else will come along and just get it. They would never get their stuff back. I stayed a week and a half without ever moving away from my tree and my things. One person would go and get food. Say, if it's kids, like, or a man or a woman, they will go and bring something back for everyone. They beg and steal, a little bit of both. Sell drugs, too. In the park. The police don't think too much of it, especially when it's the homeless people. They don't think we are selling drugs. [This is the first time Lisa has included herself in the community of homeless people.] There's a lot of prostitution as well, out there. I never prostituted, but I do feel it's dangerous, because they never know who they're getting into a car with. After a week and a half, and then staying with friends, I got tired of laying my head here, so I went to an Evanston shelter, and they brought me here. That was less than two weeks ago. I'm with Mrs. Crockett now.[2] She's helping me to get on my feet, showing me around and stuff."

Her story up to date, Lisa now allows questions: about her first night at the shelter, and about whether she and I had met somewhere before. She laughs: "Yes! I peeled potatoes with you in the kitchen, about my third night! I remember: I was scared that first night. I ain't ever been in a shelter, and I thought all the women would be hollerin' and shoutin' at each other. I couldn't go to sleep that night. I thought someone might do something to me. Then, I'm thinking about me: what's happening to me? I'm asking God, 'Why me?' I'm not angry with God; I'm angry with me. Not with my brothers and sisters. Why should I be? I put myself in this situation. If I'd gone to school and finished college and did what I had to do, I wouldn't be in this situation now. The basic reason I'm homeless is because I ain't got no job. They laid me off. I don't have any real friends: if people offer you drugs or alcohol, or you have to bring drugs or alcohol to stay, they ain't your friends. It's depressing. It's hard. I don't trust anyone in the shelter. When a person says they cannot trust themselves, how can I trust them? I don't see honesty. I sleep on my stuff: clothes, IDs and stuff. There's enough. We wash at Sarah's Circle, Mondays and Fridays. And I go to the Salvation Army. What I hate the most is the trail: just walking from shelter to shelter. Every day. Every night. But I'm going to try to keep surviving..."

After transcribing this remarkable woman's short, bleak, and heartbreaking story, I wrote the following reminder to myself: "If I am ever truly converted, this woman's strength of character will certainly have contributed to it." It remains true.

9

JANET

Just when you think you've heard it all... After being at the shelter for several years, and collecting many stories, it would be reasonable to think one had a representative sample, a well-rounded notion of the sociology and psychology of homelessness, and an understanding of victims and survivors. But there is deep truth in the paradox that human beings are simultaneously all the same and all different. No amount of story-gathering exhausts the range of human experience, degradation, and heroism. Every story stands alone; each contributes another unique and noninterchangeable piece to the great puzzle.

Janet is one of relatively few white women at the shelter. She is anxious to give me a fairly comprehensive picture of her background and circumstances. "My name is Janet Marie Hofer. I was born in Pittsburgh, Pennsylvania. When I was ten days old my mother took me to the hospital because I was having seizures— and she never came back. Much later I discovered that I ended up in a foster home for three months. Then I was given to another family, the Hofers, who eventually adopted me when I was about three. I was physically and emotionally abused by them. I have two other adopted sisters, much older than me. They are full siblings, and also adopted by the Hofers. One is in Washington state now and one in Las Vegas. I keep in touch, but I am basically the black sheep because they found their own birth family and they get family reunions and all that kind of stuff. So I'm kind of left out."

Janet sees herself as abandoned, given away, incorporated into a surrogate family, isolated, and alienated from adoptive parents and adopted sisters. It is a fragile identity on which to build a life, and the very people who could have given her a second start were responsible for her accumulating problems.

"The Hofers had no children of their own. They became foster parents through the Department of Human Services [DHS]. I finally moved out when I was twenty-one. I was being abused. My first memory of that was when I was...old enough to walk. Maybe two. My mother was chasing me around the kitchen with a butcher knife. I backed up against the wall and put out a hand to protect me, and the knife landed right there. [She shows a very ugly scar.] My next memory is, we had a vacation cabin in Maryland, and there was a beehive in the ground. I must have been defying my mother. I was maybe three. I was wearing a bathing suit, and she sat me on the beehive and held me there, because I was being a 'bad girl.' I had bee stings all over me. I remember crying in the kitchen, and she wouldn't take me to the hospital. A neighbor took me.

"She would always yell at me: 'You're a worthless person. We should have just left you there to rot.' That kind of stuff. When I was thirteen she tried to convince me to commit suicide. When I wouldn't do it, she got a razor blade and started to do it for me. But one of the worst things: indirectly, she killed my boyfriend. She was racist and he was black, so we had to keep it a secret. But she found out. I was fifteen. My boyfriend was the first person I told I was being abused, and he was like, 'I don't want to hear it; I'm getting you out of here.' So he was going to take me and run off. Like, elope. The night before, he got killed in a motorcycle accident. A couple of days later I heard a phone conversation with my mother: she put somebody up to it. When I heard that, I went to the police and told them. Smart police that they were, they went to her and said, 'Your daughter said so and so.' She convinced them that I was the one who did it. I ended up in a mental hospital. I was on Thorazine, and pretty much out of it. Years later, through regressive therapy, I remembered that I was raped in that mental hospital by an orderly."

This *is Janet's truth,* never shared with anyone. She never had the opportunity to lay it out, allowing the pieces to dovetail together. She is only thirty, and her story is not locked in some distant past. But she is trapped in a reality from which she feels there is neither escape nor redress. She is living in a nightmare, and must feel terribly claustrophobic and powerless. She knows she has some mental sickness, but that she is not "mental": she is quite lucid, and even more frustrated by that fact. She talks candidly about her medical history, reminding me of the founder of my own community, Francis Libermann (1802–1852) who suffered from epilepsy and great misunderstanding.

"I wouldn't have 'pet mals' [petit mal seizures]. I had epilepsy. But I've had less than a dozen seizures in my entire life. I was on medication, till I was about eighteen. No medication since then. I would just pass out for about ten seconds and then be all right. I'm off medication totally."

What else does she remember about life as an adopted child? "My father just sat back and agreed with everything my mother did. They were just mean. I have no idea why they would adopt kids. My oldest sister went in the Army and was sent overseas. The other one moved out and got married. I was still in first grade. There was no one else there. But the older sisters knew: they went through it too. But they were seven or eight when they were adopted. I think their own [step] mother died. Anyway, my father never intervened. He added to the fire. He always backed her up. My mother is now dead. She was sixty-something. My father is like, ninety, now. He was getting ready to retire when I was adopted. He drank a lot, and sometimes he would hit me. But most of the time, and when he was sober, he just followed what she did.

"There was not much privacy. When we were in Pennsylvania, a lot of times they would just lock me in the basement. The longest was three days. I don't know why it was not found out. They just left me. I cried most of the time. It would have been around kindergarten through second grade. Then they would just say, 'OK, it's time for you to come out now.' Sometimes they would let me eat, then. But it wasn't like, 'Oh you did this, and you have to go to the basement.' They didn't give explanations or instructions. It was not even like a psunishment. There was nothing I did to provoke it. I remember hearing noise, so I think they were still in the house. Maybe not all the time. From the age of sixteen to when I was twenty, I tried to commit suicide eight times. Razor blades. Sleeping pills. I was in a coma for eight days once! Pretty close to dying. I think the police found me. When I came out of it, I just felt worse: 'Jeez; I can't even do that right!' But it's hard to explain what goes on in your mind. But I haven't attempted suicide for ten years. It was always over the counter stuff: nonprescription."

What was her parents' reaction? She laughs: "They weren't concerned! They would say, 'Try harder next time!' I don't know why I stayed, but I did, until I was twenty-one. They finally kicked me out. I guess they just felt like it. After I left, it was great. I drove from Florida to Washington state, to my sisters'. I stayed for six months, until I got a job."

There seems to be a missing piece. She talked briefly about a boyfriend. Was there any other happy time? "That's a tough question. I had one friend up the street. Maybe I can call that my haven. I could go up there and they would feed me and treat me like family. Without that, I don't know what would have happened. A lot of people were just afraid of my mother. She was outright vicious. She wasn't one thing in private and another in public: she was mean all the time. I don't know why.

"I graduated from high school, then went to technical school for two years, for computers. I've worked everywhere: courthouse, construction, hospitals, welfare, financial brokerage firm, engineering. It's been bad luck, I guess. Either the position has been eliminated, someone's harassing me, or...It's always something. I *hope it's not me!* I think it's just bad luck. I've been sexually harassed. In my last job, the supervisor would always pick on me and tell me I was a bad person. It had nothing to do with my job. I was always getting pats on the back, and they would bring me presents—not from her—but that went on for more than a year. Nobody would believe me. That's very frustrating. I mean, what can you do? You can't control the way people think!"

Janet is agitated now. She really wants my acceptance and approval, yet recalling her own story, she finds herself revisiting buried skeletons. Nor will she be comforted by me. She wants to talk about her own search. "In 1993 I was in Seattle, homeless. I found my birth family; that's why I moved to Pittsburgh later. What a big mistake that was! My birth mother was an ex-prostitute and proud of it. Not a good person. After you had been with her you felt you needed to take a bath. I lived with her, and I have a half sister. She was thirteen then, about ten years younger than me. She was an active gang member, and just really mean. Also I have a full sister and a full brother who don't believe I am their real sister. My mother was with my father for a while."

This is so complicated, messy, and bizarre: a prostitute mother having multiple babies, apparently by one man, yet still doing prostitution. Did Janet ever figure that out? "Yeah. Well. My older sister, Diane, I think she's the product of another man. She doesn't look like anybody. My other sister is probably brain damaged because my mother and father put tape over her nose and mouth because she wouldn't stop crying. She was an infant. That was in my medical record. I don't know why I remember that my adopted sisters remembered my original last name [Martindale], and I knew I was at a certain hospital. I requested my medical records from that hospital, so I discovered where I was born. The birth records used three different last names—Martindale, Korack [my dad's name], and Erit, which I thought was my father's last name, because that was on the medical record, because I'm the youngest of that litter, and because when I was born my mother was with someone else, and she was afraid of my natural father because he used to beat her up. I wrote to my mother about five years ago."

Although this does not make much sense to me, people don't just imagine this kind of stuff. It means something to Janet, even though she is not altogether clear just what. It is her truth, her assembling of the puzzle of her life. But exactly how did she become homeless?

"It was about five years ago. I had been working in a lawyer's office for three years. They got a new manager who sexually harassed me. It was words more than anything. He would say, 'If you want a raise you're going to have to...' whatever. It wasn't a joke. It was disgusting. I called the supervisor, and three higher-up supervisors, and they all told me, 'If you don't like it, you can leave.' After another year and a half I finally quit, couldn't find another job, couldn't pay the rent, and got evicted. So I was in a shelter, in Seattle. That was scary. Terrifying. When I knew I was going to get evicted, I went to the welfare office, and they gave me some food stamps and a list of shelters. I checked them out, and found the only one with any free beds. The landlord must have taken all my stuff. I had just a couple of suitcases of clothes. At the Union Gospel Mission, you got your own room: a locked room where you could store stuff. I stayed maybe a month. During that month I found my birth family in Pittsburgh.

"My blood brother (in Pittsburgh) paid for a bus ticket for me to go out there. He didn't know about me until then, and we had not even met. My birth mother gave each of us away almost as soon as she had us. She kept my oldest sister for a while, and then she told social services to come get her. My brother she left on a doorstep and me she abandoned at the hospital. So we were all separated. But by this time, both of them had been looking for me. It was a happy day when I went to Pittsburgh. But when I got there I just had the feeling that I'd made this big mistake. My sister was very casual with me. She is married with two kids, and the person she is married to is not the father of either of the kids, and only one of the kids is living with her. My brother is gay and I think he lives with somebody. I haven't talked to him in a long time. Anyway, I lived with my grandfather for maybe a week, in this small town in Ohio. I don't remember how they found him. He was OK. He tried to help me out. He bought me clothes and made sure I had food. He was divorced and remarried, with two kids living with him. One was his natural daughter, Maxine, my aunt. The other was a boy of twelve or thirteen, Roger, who was adopted, I think.

"At this point I still haven't met my birth mother in Pittsburgh, and there was nowhere for me to get a job. My siblings take me to Pittsburgh, and I meet my birth mother and my half sister. I'm feeling excited, but now…I don't know. I want this to work. But it was hard to tell if she was glad to see me. I don't know if she ever really worked in her life. She always got disability [SSI], because something was wrong with her knee. She walked with a cane. She was in her late forties. She's dead now. She died—of cancer in her kidneys. She was a little taller than me, about 350 pounds,[1] red hair. She doesn't look like me; I look more like my dad. I lived with her about six months. She was lazy, no conscience, could be really mean, didn't care about anything. She didn't seem to care about me. I asked her what had happened way back, and she just told me that she took me to the hospital and didn't go back. She didn't say why—but my medical records say I was having seizures.

"She said someone threatened to tell that I was living with her, and that she would be cut off welfare. But I don't think that happened. She said, 'So you've got to leave now.' So I left. I rented a room for more than two years. Then I met a boyfriend and moved in with him. That didn't work out [she laughs nervously, but does not elaborate], but I lived there for nine months before moving again, into my own apartment in Pittsburgh, and lived there for another year. While I was living with my boyfriend I was harassed by that human resources lady. So I quit in January last year, and until October I was working through temp agencies. In

November I had no work, and I got evicted in February—last month—for the second time. I moved here about six weeks ago, because I had met a few people from here—on the Internet. I haven't made contact with them yet. A friend in Nashville got me a bus ticket, and then I called an 800 number for shelters. They just came and got me, and took me to the Salvation Army. A case worker there told me about REST. I've been here every night since."

Janet seems familiar with the system and willing to conform to expectations. But at what cost to her self-respect? And what about her job prospects?

"I haven't found a job yet. It's a 'catch 22,' because no one will give me the bus fare to go for an interview, and I don't have anywhere to keep my stuff if I leave it. Maybe my friend in Nashville will help. I have NOTHING! And I can't get public assistance because I don't have an Illinois ID. They said I could go to Truman College and do my resumé, so I did that. Then I will go to the library, check the Sunday paper, and write down the jobs I'm going to apply for. That's all helpful to me.[2] I do feel grateful for the shelter, that I don't have to sleep on the sidewalk. That happened to me in Pittsburgh for three days. The shelter there was full. It's real scary being on the streets. Near the broker's where I was working, there was a little alley, and I stayed there. Nobody bothered me. I didn't have a sleeping bag. Just sat in the alley and tried to sleep. Another time I was in a shelter in Seattle for a month, but this shelter is much better. It's just nice to be inside. I don't think it matters what color you are, but there are problems. This morning there was almost a big fight. This lady wouldn't get up, and when the supervisor tried to rouse her, she just said, 'F… you!' Then she and another lady got into a fight and almost started throwing chairs at each other. So the police were called, and one of them got taken out. It just seems that everywhere you go, there's a fight. Everywhere you go."

Keen and telling reflections; true and bleak words. It is very difficult and challenging to listen to. How does one hold on to sanity? How does one formulate any plans? Janet immediately brightens:

"I want to get a job, and an apartment, so that I can get out of here. As soon as possible! Within the next two weeks. I haven't thought about suicide for several years. Ten years ago, when I moved to Seattle, there was a test program for people who were depressed. The treatment was free, at the University of Washington. It worked for me. I have something to live for now. I don't want to die! To get a job, and get out of here: that's good enough for me. Still, I don't have an Illinois ID, and no money to get one. It's about ten dollars, and you have to go downtown."

Janet is not begging, or pleading, or even promising. She is just stating the facts. Can she come up with ten dollars? It doesn't seem that much. To me. "No. How? Where? I won't beg. I don't do that. And I don't steal. It's not right."

Where does "right" come in: doesn't she think she has been treated abysmally? Doesn't that give her certain rights? She says, quietly and firmly, "No! It doesn't matter what people have done. It's not right to steal." But where did she get this conviction, this strong sense of what is right and what is not? By her answer, I know she is not trying to impress me.

"I don't know. It's a good question. *NOT* from my mother! But it's very strong. Very! The worst thing I ever did? When I was young, I used to sneak out of the window to see my boyfriend. I don't know if that was the worst—baddest—thing. The best—goodest—thing? I was walking down the street in Seattle, and I found twenty dollars on the ground. I had maybe fifty dollars in my pocket at the time. This man was walking down the street, and he looked real haggard, real hungry. And he said, 'Can you spare a dollar so that I can get something to eat?' And I said, 'Here you go! And I gave him the twenty dollars.'" She laughs with glee at this happy memory.

The homeless population is fluid. Some people move on. Some move out. Some actually succeed in getting a job and an apartment, though the odds are stacked against them. Those who take advantage of a case worker have the best chance. Janet seemed very strongly motivated.

I thanked her for her time and candor, and gave her twenty dollars for her ID. She was overwhelmed. I wished her well, and hoped she would make it. The following week, I saw her again at the shelter, and Janet proudly showed me her new Illinois ID! Since then, I only saw her once. I hope she made it. She certainly deserved to.

10

DEBORAH

Some women begin with a trickle of words; others are direct and to the point. One April day, Deborah took her time and made herself comfortable, and then suddenly launched straight into her story. "I am Deborah Wynn, and I was born in Evanston. My folks came from Iowa. I have three sisters and one brother. I did have another brother, but he drowned at age seventeen, on a fishing trip. I am the last and the youngest. My childhood was pretty much happy. My dad's dead now. He died of cancer, but he and my mother were together until then. That was 1985. I was twenty-one then.[1] I was at home when he died."

Deborah is controlled and punctilious: she prides herself on details and on judgment. Will she talk about her childhood? "I think it was just an ordinary childhood. I was the baby. I went to school and graduated high school, then worked at a Jewel store for a couple of years. After that, everything went crazy. Mostly it was money situations. My father left me (the youngest) his Social Security income. Somehow my mother got hold of it—secretly: Can you do that?—and had it put in her name. Maybe seven hundred dollars a month. He had been a carpenter. My mother gets it even now. That money was for my support. The others had jobs and money. And for fifteen years [later she will modify this] I've been on the streets. One reason I couldn't get a job was because I didn't have an ID, which I really do not need to get if I'm down here. Don't you have to change your address and ID? I don't even have an ID for Zion [forty miles north] now. That expired five years ago. I lost it. My mom had it and she lost it."

In less than five minutes, Deborah seems to have suffered a kind of meltdown. She is babbling, talking almost incoherently. Yet she will not stop and gather her wits. She blunders on: "I had a case worker at the Salvation Army. I have one here at the shelter. I look for jobs. Like today. I'm going to McDonald's to look. In fifteen years I've had one, two jobs. Not much. Very little money. My father left me income. That's the trouble. It ain't easy to survive."

Deborah still has not elaborated on the story of her childhood. Memory of her mother's perfidy now dominates her mental horizon. Later, she acknowledges that she was always "slow" and that she had some major learning difficulties [which are not immediately apparent]. She intimated that she did not get a job because that might have cut her off from Social Security—but she was not even on Social Security! "Yes I was!" she expostulated, "and my mother got her name on the check."

It is clearer now that Deborah is living in the past, feeding on her anger and frustration at her mother. "I talk to my mom and ask her to send money. She gives me delays: she says I have to wait until she gets it... One sister lives in Pennsylvania. A brother lives in Georgia. [Indignantly now:] Nothing's stopping me from getting a job! I do want to work! But I'm kinda tired not having any money. I think I need someone to help me out with goals. I don't do drugs or alcohol. None of that. I don't have any mental problems. But my mother said I am slow. The [Illinois] State people think that. I think I'm pretty smart. I don't know what has happened in the past fifteen years."

Now she is trying to link her childhood to her present circumstances: "No bad experiences, with boyfriends or anything. Just that life has not been put together. I'm still trying to figure out what happened. Other people have their own problems. But I can get clothes and stuff. At Sarah's Circle."

She was drifting and became incoherent. We change the subject. She had initially said she had been homeless for fifteen years, but now she tells a different story: "It's about two years ago." Then, confused, she rethinks. "No, things started happening around the house when I was twenty-one, but I left when I was thirty-four. My mother was looking after me. My twin sister was there too. She works in Skokie, Illinois. [Previously, with no mention of a twin, she had simply said she was the youngest of the family.] My mother was doing the cooking and stuff. She bought my clothes. I just walked out when there was nothing for me there. I had a job, at Jewel's [but this was long before, I thought]. I did volunteer work at Great America. My mom was OK. The money was for looking after me anyhow.

"I was in special education at school [and she graduated from special ed]. I could read! They just said I was slow. I asked around, on the street, for a shelter. The end of 1997. They gave me an orientation, told me to get a TB test, and I've been here ever since. I keep pretty much to myself. It's fine with me. I don't mess with people and they don't mess with me. At first, it was hard getting used to—listening to those women who swear! They were high. I never did any of that, or drank, when I was growing up. That's what killed my daddy. He would drink a lot. He didn't beat me. He got outta hand sometimes. He never hit me. But he beat my mother. He hit one of my sisters. No one ever gave me any trouble, even on the streets."

This woman is evidently mentally unbalanced, yet lucid and articulate enough to tell her story—which comes through with all the hallmarks of mental illness. This is neither totally incoherent nor completely coherent, but a strange mixture. She dwells in an "empty home." It is bleak and very sad, for here is a woman who has no recourse and no realistic expectation of improvement. She has experienced the drowning death of a brother when she was only ten, a mother whom she feels has betrayed her, and a father who was a violent alcoholic. No wonder she feels disconnected and uncherished. Is there anyone at all in her life now…a boyfriend, perhaps? "Uh, uh... No. No, I'm probably not ready for a relationship yet. I'd like one. I guess. Sometimes, yes. All I want now is to get a job. Get a place to stay. It's been fifteen years... I'll give it a shot. I really don't know..." She has drifted away again.

Does she think of anything in particular during the long days on the streets, her family or her home? "Yes. I do. And I have some contact with my brothers and sisters. They don't really help me much. We were close, once. My mother would read us the Bible every day. We went to the Baptist church every week. I pray. Jesus is close."

Deborah seems increasingly distracted and on edge, so I ask her about her ambition, and indicate that this will be the final question. Like so many other women, but perhaps even more surprising than almost all of them (who are less obviously mentally impaired), Deborah is quick to identify that she really does have something to live for.

"I'm hoping to improve myself so I can get out of the shelter. It's not a permanent thing, to stay there. I'm going to work on my goals, and pray more. Life is OK. I'd like it to get better, not worse. I never get arrested, or roughed up, or abused on the streets. I'm a cardholder at REST, so I always get a bed at the shelter. I keep going to meetings. You have to attend five a week, to keep your status: housing groups, AA meetings, art class, community group. You can attend two a day. At one o'clock I'll go over to McDonald's and try for a job."

Deborah collects her few things, wraps herself in her dignity, smiles wanly, and sets off through the streets of Uptown, vaguely in the direction of McDonald's, mecca of the homeless, the cold, and the abandoned. How can she possibly have managed all these years? Perhaps her mental impairment actually helps her survival, sealing her off from too much reality. But there must be much more to it than that: the spark of hope has not yet been utterly extinguished.

There was another woman, years before, whose conversation

was not taped. She talked for maybe fifteen minutes, about a series of awful, unmitigated disasters and injustices in her life. It was appalling. So I asked, very quietly, why she had not just ended it all, jumped off a bridge or under a train. With a look of incredulity, she said, with more excitement than she had shown in the previous quarter hour, with a sense that what she was saying was completely self-evident, and with emphasis on the verb rather than the noun—"You *gotta* have hope, Tony!! You *gotta* have hope!"

Sometimes there *is* life without hope, and that equates to the despair that drives people over the edge. So, the maxim "where there's life, there's hope" is simply not always true. But where hope survives, life continues. Deborah, for some unfathomable and inscrutable reasons, continues to live in hope: and where there's hope, there's life.

11

JANICE

It is November, and winter is approaching implacably. Three weeks previously, an event has shaken up the homeless women, and I need to know more. I was out of town at the time and had missed the whole drama. It concerns two of the women whose stories are recounted earlier: Brenda (chapter 4) and her partner Darla (chapter 5). Today Janice, a friend of both women, is with me. Before we get into her story, I ask her to tell me more.

"It was Thursday morning [three weeks before], and Darla was crying in the shelter. We asked her what was wrong. She said the police found Brenda's body that morning. She took it real hard. Brenda's parents were deceased. It was real sad. Her three children were at the funeral. They were going to cremate her, but the pastor gave her a funeral.[1] They found a nice dress for her. The embalming fluid made her look real dark, but she was high yellow when she was alive. She looked just like she was sleeping."

Later, at home, I reread Brenda's story, noting her hopes, her faith in God, and her statement that within a year she wanted to be clean, sober, in an apartment, and reunited with her children. A year to the day, she would be dead and buried. Janice has details: "Brenda's body was found in an alley. The police found another lady in the same alley on the same day. Brenda had been strangled, bludgeoned, raped, and stabbed upwards of seventeen times in her private parts. The funeral was right here in Uptown Ministries. Brenda's son signed for the body. Her daughter found out on the evening news. It was very sad. But as my mother used to say, 'You enjoy the day, because you don't know what will come.' This makes the women very scared, especially women who, you know, do get into cars and such. But it's very hard. I know a lot of women who have dated, the guy gave her the money, did what he wanted to do with her, then beat her up and took the money back. They found another woman in the garbage with her throat cut, one in an abandoned building, and one more down the street in an abandoned garage. All in one week. One woman escaped and got to the police. She described a guy who stopped her and asked her if she smoked. She said yes, and he started stabbing her. She thanked the Lord that she was able to run right out. She got to somebody's house and they called the police."

These revelations pour from Janice like a torrent. Only later will I be able to reflect on Brenda—her life, her smile, her helpful presence in the kitchen, her survival against the odds—and on the unspeakable indignity and horror of her death. Before me as I write this, is Brenda's printed funeral service, with her photograph: Brenda posed, smiling, wistful yet hopeful... She was thirty-five years old, and the obituary reads:

> Brenda Graham...attended DuSable High School. She accepted Christ at Chicago Uptown Ministry. Brenda was outgoing and a very outstanding person. She got along with everybody and she loved to laugh and joke around. Brenda departed this life Saturday, October 30, 1999. Her mother and father preceded her in death. She leaves to cherish her memory L. C., Ruby, Devon, and Sergio Graham; brothers James and Willie Daniels; mother-in-law Essie D. Daniels; sisters-in-law Georgia, Ethel, and Essie; brother-in-law Melvin Daniels; and a host of relatives and friends whom all loved her dearly.

It is well-intentioned and carefully constructed; but it has a hollow ring for those who actually knew Brenda. May she rest in peace.

But Janice is anxious to tell me her own story: "My name is Janice Bibbs. I was born in Chicago. My parents stayed together in a common-law marriage. There were six kids. Three deceased: one (sister) died in childhood; one was killed [murdered]; and another brother died in the service—in a plane crash, I think."

Janice has suffered. Yet again there is an absence of self-pity common to so many of the women: "I can't complain about my childhood. I guess I was the spoiled brat because I was the baby. My mother was a correctional officer for twenty-four years, and she worked nights. So I was brought up by her mother. My mother and me would go shopping when she came home, and fishing when we went on vacation. My father was a good dad. He would whup me when I did bad things—but not beat me. Half the time, I was only on punishment for a minute, because he couldn't stay mad with me. I love my father, but I loved my mother more. It's been ten years since he passed. My mother passed last year.

"We used to go to church. Oh yes! Every week. It was a Baptist church. I stopped when I was in my teens, when I got old enough to say I didn't want to go. I just wanted to hang out with my girlfriends and do our makeup or go to a show or a game—and stay out late. I'm forty now. I guess I started to come back in my middle thirties."

Janice is cheerful, realistic, in touch with reality and battle-scarred. Not only does she not complain, she appears to accept much of the blame. She sketches the broad lines of her youth, indicating how her life began to unravel.

"I had a year and a half of college. But I went through a bad depression then. I had a baby son at the time. I was with his father, but we broke up. He moved out. I couldn't afford to pay the rent after that, and my mother couldn't help. So I moved back with my mother. I quit college and did all kinds of security jobs, but I messed up. My employers promised to keep my job open if I went on a program. My mother said she would look after the baby.

"But then I started on drugs. Reefer, snorting cocaine, then smoking cocaine. I was doing so much it nearly brought me down. But I stopped! For a whole year! Then treatment. Then clean for six months. But now I understand that you need to be with positive people or you will [backslide]. But I never had that understanding at that time. My sponsor told me that.

"I always kept a job, but I was borrowing money. I didn't have to sell my body for it. I was using forty or fifty dollars a day. When you start, you're doing it all day, all day. When I had the money I would go the whole nine yards, but when I don't have the money..." Janice is suddenly disconnected, imprisoned by memories. Then she comes back to the present.

"The worst time was when I got several income-tax checks. Easy money! But I blew [the last one]: every dime! I was doing drugs. But the lowest thing, the thing I really regret...was when I stole...things from my mother's house." Janice is sobbing now, deep, heaving convulsive sighs and whimpers. It is overwhelming, and she is ashamed.

"This was about 1992. She died in 1998. I stole her microwave, her carpet cleaner... She had a bill to pay. She had excellent credit and she could get anything she wanted. She had three thousand dollars. I knew she had it in her purse, and I stole it. She was so hurt. She cried...Another time I took her credit card and charged all kinds of things. But she forgave me." Again Janice breaks down. Again she controls herself and continues: "My brothers and sisters were saying to my mother, 'You should put that bitch out.' But she said, 'She needs my help; that's my child.' And I kept on. But after a while I did stop and went for treatment. I was out of control. I just didn't know how to stop or where to turn. I started calling [telephone] hot-lines. I went to AA detox for twenty-eight days. It worked for me. I found that you can actually go to the store without stealing, and you can go out and have fun without getting high. I was clean for up to six months. That was the longest until now. I have been clean now for two months."

Listening to the women's stories is a reminder of just how difficult true conversion is. People like Janice—falling, getting up, and continuing time after time—live truly heroic lives. They have so little help, often such a poor self-image, and so many "temptations" against which to struggle. Where there's hope, there's life: but it can be difficult to understand the source of many women's hope. Their courage in the face of such odds is amazing, their lack of bitterness is awesome.

Janice talks candidly and unselfconsciously about her experience in the shelter and her hopes. "I have been here about three weeks. I had been staying with people but, you know, they put you out. My son is twenty-one and he is in Des Plaines, Illinois. I am with a man now. He's out there. We've been together three and a half years [even though] he could stay with his mother. We are trying to get a place, but we're trying to organize our personal stuff before we move in. I don't have a job. I've been trying to work on my...there's a lot of things been bugging me. I try to go to three meetings a day. I get SSI. I hope I will be able to get a job. I get four hundred ninety-five dollars; that's basically my rent, but I have been trying to make a security down payment on my house. All the money goes into that, except thirty dollars."

Janice's dogged determination is impressive. But how can she raise her current income and secure her house? Perhaps she steals or begs, or prostitutes? She is quite indignant as she replies: "No! I eat at the Salvation Army, Sarah's Circle, and places like that. I don't need money. I don't want money right now."

And how did she feel the first time at the shelter? "I felt ashamed. Hurt. A bit afraid. When you're used to having your own place...and you can't sleep with the noise, or the thought that people are going through your bag...It's kind of hard. But I'm a cardholder now. I have a case worker. I'm pretty satisfied with the shelter. You don't have to sleep on the street. It's somewhere you can come and at least shower and sleep and eat. But some of the women come in and they don't want to get a shower... but then, who am I to judge? I worry about myself and I don't tell other people what to do. I'm on a schedule. I know what to do when I go to the shelter."

Such clarity of purpose, forbearance, and commitment! Janice's conversation now turns quite naturally to God (chapter 13). My final questions concern Janice's reasons for coming to talk with me in the first place, and her hopes for the future. "I like the fact that some people listen. Also, it's good for me to get some stuff off my chest. I did it once before. It helps me to focus. The future? I'm looking forward to moving my furniture [she laughs]. I mean, when I get it! But I hope I'll be in an apartment soon. A job is not so important. I have to deal with my own personal stuff first."

And that is it. Janice has said what she wants to say. Now she is ready to face the rapidly advancing winter, to get on with her life, and to deal with her own personal stuff. A woman of courage and dignity, she knows how difficult life is: it was she who told me about Brenda's terrible death. She says a pleasant goodbye—until we meet again at the shelter. But we never do... I truly hope Janice dealt successfully with her personal stuff—and got to move her furniture into an apartment of her own.

12

LORRAINE

She walked into the shelter one night: a lonely old woman without a roof, without friends, and without, it seemed, a history. Just Lorraine. She came night after night, was unfailingly courteous, but never volunteered any personal information. One day, after almost a year, she said she wanted to talk about her life. A week later, we set up a meeting: the usual place, the usual conditions. Lorraine evidently had a plan, and she began to talk.

"My name is Lorraine Speredes. My father was Greek. I was born in Evanston, Illinois. Father had a restaurant in Wilmette, Illinois, and we lived there. I had a brother and a sister. My mother and father are deceased. I was born in 1925 [it is now 2000]. I had a very happy life. My father was strict, and I listened to him. Today people don't listen to parents. They're just trying to put their parents in jail. And the parents are only trying to help the kids. My mother and father were very nice people. Father was a family man. He stuck to the family. And his father and mother were always close—to each other and to us. I was raised and baptized Greek Orthodox. I went to high school for four years, and then I got a job, making walkie-talkies for the war. That was around 1940.

"I liked anything to do with nursing: nursing companioning. I liked to take care of people. I got married and had a daughter and a son. I broke up with him when the kids were little. I had trouble with him. He wanted me to move out of state, but I said I would rather stay with my mother. I was close to her, so I stayed. He left. He didn't want to stay. He did support me when he left for California. I got a divorce but never remarried.

"My daughter married when she was seventeen and has two boys. I'm still in touch. My son was moving to California from his apartment, and he said he wanted me to move with him. But I didn't go. I had an apartment. But then they tore it down. That's why I'm in the shelter. I came here nearly a year ago, and was in The Cornerstone first. But they closed. Anyway, I was working. Companioning. And I worked in a factory about five years. I didn't retire. I got unemployment about three years ago, and collected it for a year and a half. Then I got off it. The state dropped me.[1] You can't get anymore, and I didn't have any insurance. Well, my daughter didn't do much. She just said, 'You'll have to look for another apartment.' I looked for a lot of apartments. I had social workers helping. But when you put your name on the list, you just have to wait. My son knows I'm in the shelter. He is sad. He said I should try to look around. But he's in California. He'll probably come back sometime."

Lorraine has two adult children with money, and they just tell their mother to look for a place! Meanwhile she is abjectly poor and living in a shelter—and not even *living* in a shelter, because she is on the street between 7:00 AM and 8:00 PM. How does she feel, virtually abandoned in her seventies?

"I'm not angry or upset at others, because I don't want to depend on anyone. If I depend on myself it gives me a stronger will to manage. Then I can't say I can't do it because I don't have someone to help me. I think I can get some companion work."

Lorraine is sparrowlike: small, thin, and nervously alert. She has always been bright and friendly, and she invariably calls me by name, although she has no small talk and never gets drawn into conversation with anyone. She seems self-disciplined and self-contained, which is how she said she was raised. But, given that she was relatively comfortable and secure until the age of seventy-five, when she became a homeless person almost overnight, her resilience and apparent equanimity are astonishing. Is there some deep, inner place to which she withdraws, where she can shut out the outside world in order to carry on living her solitary life? Some of the women say that she is a bit strange, but they do not elaborate. She explains her attitude.

"I never thought I'd be in a shelter. I never even heard much about shelters. The first night, some of the women were rowdy. I thought the best thing to do was just to say hello and goodbye, and I never had anything else to do with them. I just didn't have much preparation for being in a shelter. When they tore my building down, they gave us very little notice. I didn't even know where I'd be that night. I thought I'd get a hotel nearby. But the two hotels in my neighborhood were torn down at the same time! The city said they would try to help me find a place, but they never did. I could find places, but the prices were so high! I was paying six hundred twenty-five dollars a month, with little money left over for food. Now I have seven hundred dollars from Social Security, and I just can't get a place and food as well. The rooms went up to forty-three dollars a day, and I used to pay twenty dollars! My brother in Evanston said they had a shelter there. I stayed there for a while. My brother has a house, but no room for me. He has a wife and two boys and grandchildren. It didn't really bother me at all [that he didn't take me in]. I always say people have to do what they want to do. It didn't bother me at all. He doesn't know that I'm here, but he did ask to know where I am.

"The first night in the shelter, we had this lady, Kathleen. She made me feel very comfortable. She told me there were some seniors' buildings that I might be able to get into. I wasn't afraid. I do want to get an apartment, one that's reasonable. I'm starting to look, and I'm looking for a job, too. Some of my possessions are in storage. I don't get assistance from REST, and I can probably do better on my own [than expect someone to find me a job]. If I can put an ad in the local paper, Sarah's will give me a postal address.[2] I have to come to REST for meetings [to ensure her "good standing"—assurance of a place in the shelter]. I started out with ten sessions, and did those. Then I got my card. Now I have to do another twenty sessions—AA, artwork, anything. I don't drink, but I wanted to see how other people are doing, how they are coping with life. I've never been to those meetings before. I went to NA [Narcotics Anonymous], the cocaine meetings, as well."

Lorraine is focused and positive. "Society" assumes she must be feckless, abused, or addicted, because she has no home. She seems unconcerned: "It doesn't bother me! I always said that everyone is responsible for what they do. In the meetings they ask me questions about myself. I say all my actions are up to me. If you don't follow your instincts and do the right thing, you're going to get into trouble with the law and with yourself. Nothing bothers me! I never get depressed! A lot of people in the shelter are depressed because they don't seem like they're going anywhere. They talk about going somewhere but they're not. I'm trying to get a job. I want to get a job."

But don't many women want a job? Lorraine disagrees: despite what they say, they don't really. She also insists that some people worry too much: she sees life in very simple terms. But doesn't temperament play a significant part in people's survival? Some are anxious, and seem to crumble and soon disappear from the shelter. Lorraine, however, shows up week after week. Though she does not have a job, nor is she depressed. There must be other issues, some unfathomable. I begin to tell Lorraine that I do not think I could survive on the streets. But she responds—typically—by reverting to her own story: she has little capacity for empathy or for dialogue.

"Oh, I worry sometimes, and I think, 'Well, this really isn't my style; this isn't for me.' But I don't worry every day. I just take one day at a time. It doesn't depress me because eventually I'll get out of here, get a job, and leave."

Hope, it appears, springs eternal. But isn't she afraid of the violence? "No. Because I don't talk to people much. I found out the less you talk to people, the better you are. I just go on and do my business. I've never been mugged. I don't ask for money. I know some people...I don't think they are dealing with a full deck, you know: some of them need mental help. This morning a lady got into the ladies' room. The other women were trying to get her out. She was lying down on the floor—about seven times! She told Teresa [the supervisor] she was tired! One woman threatened to hit her if she did it again. She needs help. I have never been treated for mental problems."

But something does not compute. Either Lorraine is mentally dissociating from the hard reality of her life, or...perhaps there is some form of autism—which actually makes her life easier. She does not look at the person she talks to. What does she attribute her survival to? She talks about God,[3] but also claimed to have mental stamina. "I just don't let myself get sucked into it all. I try to stay above it. I have a grandson who's fifteen, and I'd like to help him. I don't really see him, but I call him. I used to see my brother on the Fourth of July, and so on. I'm close to him and my sister..." But the conviction has gone.

Because Lorraine is white (very much in the minority), I ask for her thoughts about homeless women of other ethnicities, particularly African American women who are statistically overrepresented. Does she keep to herself because of racist tendencies? But she is open-minded and tolerant, well-disposed yet candid. "What do I feel? Well...really nothing. [African Americans] are OK if they behave themselves. Some of them don't know how. I can kind of ignore people if I don't want to get too friendly with them. I just mind my own business. You do what you gotta do, and you won't ever [need to] fight. If they want to pick a fight with you, you don't have to say nothing. I try to be friendly with everybody. Some black people [at the shelter] are prejudiced, and they say the whites are prejudiced. That's not so, because years ago when there was slavery...I said, 'You know what: I don't even want to hear about it. I was never born at that time. That's long gone.' I'm not angry. But, you know what, Tony, I believe one thing: what goes around comes around. If someone wants to hurt you, maybe *I* won't want to get back at them, but eventually it will come back to them."

Lorraine is very adroit: she could have been drawn into a heated and passionate argument, but she withdrew with dignity and self-control. That capacity—to keep her own counsel and neither to give nor take offense—has served her very well over the years. She simply will not be drawn where she does not wish to go! So I willingly give her the last word, knowing that she will deftly edit it: does she have something to look forward to?

"I want to go back to companion work, get some money, and an apartment. I hope I'm not in the shelter by the end of the year. I don't have too many plans. I will put my name in the papers [for a job]. I used to love riding my bike. If I had a bike now, I would really get around. I love to cook, too." And with those final flights of fancy, Lorraine wanders off into the late-spring morning.

Five years have passed. Lorraine came to the shelter for about three years. She was now close to eighty. Initially she was unfailingly optimistic, though she never volunteered to help, even in small ways. But as time went on, she became more distracted and distanced from everyone and everything. Some women complained that she would steal things, and for a time she was banned. Others said her personal hygiene was very bad, which made life in the shelter difficult for those in her vicinity. People said that she liked to go to the horseraces and put a bet. But for more than a year there has been no sight of, nor any information about, Lorraine. This is unusual, for the "grapevine" on the streets is particularly good.

The women assume that Lorraine, who appeared never to have done much harm to anyone, and was more sinned against than sinning, finished up alone and unloved, despite having a brother and a sister, a daughter and a son, and at least one grandchild. Like too many homeless people, she may have been discovered when she was already dead, and unceremoniously deposited in a pauper's grave in Potter's Field, where I have buried a number of people over the years. In which case, may she rest in peace.

13

AN
UNCONVENTIONAL GOD

Relationships with these women developed from a real need of my own: my religious community is committed to "the poorest and most abandoned" of people. En route back to ministry in Africa, and needing to stay close to such people, I encountered them in homeless poor women of Chicago.

Given their extraordinary experiences, I was curious to know whether God (still) figured in their lives. Every woman I interviewed had something to say about God, usually unsolicited. The individual stories and the composite picture they produce are so fascinating that I kept them until now. Taking the stories in sequence, and recapitulating some salient features of each, we are now offered an insight into their thoughts about God.

First Tina, whose grief was still raw. Mother of a murdered son, homeless, penniless, and alone, she was nevertheless not angry with God: "No. I have been. I got angry when he took my mom away. I was slightly angry when he took my son also. I figured he could have done something about it…But everyone has a time to go. In my mind, it was like God already saw my son's life, before he was born, and I guess he wanted to spare him.

God wasn't playing games, just sitting up there and saying, 'OK we are all going to have Eric shot to death.'"

This is the only time Tina named her son. She always kept his name to herself. Now she speaks about God as calling Eric by name. It is very touching. Tina, who had told me that she only managed "by the grace of God," now elaborates on her relationship with the Almighty.

"I used to blame God sometimes, saying, 'you know you could have done better for me. You could have stopped me going down that road. You could have tapped me on the shoulder and given me some kind of wakening.' But I'm not against God. My faith is getting stronger. I got hope, Tony. Just that the day will come when I have a good paying job....God is right here; he's here. He's real important...guiding me, making me believe there's something better than using drugs and being around...not bad people but people that's doing bad things. I know this because I read the Bible a lot."

What does organized religion mean to Tina? As usual, her response is forbearing and kind: "A lot of church people have done things I don't think church people should do or even think. That would make me not confident in them. I haven't actually suffered from any of them. I go to the Uptown Baptist Church all the time. I like it a lot. They know me. Now, when they see me again, clean and sober, they are happy. The pastor knows me. I have taken some of the women from the shelter there. Most of them like where they're at: they are not interested in church. I do Bible study twice a week, at Uptown Ministry and Uptown Baptist. Maybe ten people. We take a passage and we discuss it."

Tina's personal faith and trust in God are expressed in a private devotional life and a minimum of organized religion. She sees hypocrisy in the Church, yet finds the local Baptist church and its pastors very sympathetic, insightful, and relevant. Evidently religion and its ministers can either be part of a problem or part of its solution. Since Tina has not mentioned Jesus, I ask her why not. Jesus is simply irrelevant to her now. "I guess because when I was growing up I heard about God...When I pray to God, Father, Creator, I say 'thank you God for waking me up...Father God.'"

Nor does Jeanette, violently abused by several men, speak of Jesus. She says: "I believe in God. I do. I pray every night before I go to bed. If I do good or bad or right or wrong, I pray for another day. Every day I wake up I thank God for another day. Blame God for the position I'm in? Why? I can't blame God. Whatever happens is my fault—not getting thrown down the stairs, but being homeless. Yes, I need God in my life, a spiritual guide and spiritual awareness."

Prayer is significant in the life of virtually all the women. Lunette, big-hearted and proud of her homeless twenty-two-year-old son, spoke of how she managed to survive in the face of recent setbacks that broke her ordered existence wide open and almost frightened the life out of her: "I had my faith. I kept my head up, and my belief. I believe in God and I believe in God very seriously. And God kept me going. I just prayed and talked to God every day, every night. Me and my son are Catholic. We would both go to church at St. Benedict's. With him being in private school, he went to church every day. So, he came home one day, very excited, and said he wanted to join the Catholic Church and me with him. We've been in the Catholic Church since 1980. God is keeping me and my son together. There were times I wanted to give up, but God was always there. When my husband got sick I looked after both of them by myself. If I could carry the cross then, I could carry it again. Sometimes I'd be ready to give up, but God said, 'No! You're not goin' to give up. You goin' to stay here and do *my* will.' That's the feeling I get. When I talk to God I get a real good feeling. I feel better 'bout myself. It seems I want to do more and more when I talk to God. Sometimes I sit down in a corner by myself. I be by myself. I pray with the Bible and sometimes I don't. In a quite place. But I go to the Salvation Army. We used to go to St. Benedict's every Sunday, every time they had something at church. We [were] always there. I don't know any [Catholic] churches up here. St. Benedict, that's my family. They

[are] my friends. They are going to help me when I get an apartment. I know they will help me. They have always been there. They never turned their back on me."

Lunette's candidness is compelling: she speaks simply and with deep conviction, about her relationship with God, her conversations, and about how Bible-reading and private prayer constitute her spirituality. It is also encouraging to hear her endorsement of the Catholic community. Her strong, simple, profound faith shines through her testimony. She is without guile.

"What do I look forward to? I want to die a happy death, and I know I'm going to live forever in paradise. I don't worry about death, dying, or funeral. I know God won't turn his back on me, on his family. God knows he's going to be there for me. I have hope because I know God's not going to cause what I want to come, but he's always on time. He ain't never failed me, and he ain't going to fail me now. God always has been there for me, because God always gave me the strength and the courage to do his will."

In view of her violent death within the year, Brenda's reflections are particularly poignant. Living in hope, doing no harm, Brenda would be brutalized, murdered, bundled in a plastic bag, and left in a garbage bin. This is what she had told me:

"I pray to God. God is in my heart. God is very important to me. I believe in the Lord. I pick up the Bible every day and read it, but yesterday was the first time I've been to church in almost ten years. Yesterday I felt the need to start going to church. I do think God loves me. I do know that God works in mysterious ways. Nobody knows what's going to happen. I know he's a good person. He's there for me. I'm not angry at God, because he's a good God. As I'm going through all this shit again, maybe God's trying to tell me something and help me up, to give me the chance to get my life back in order again."

I wonder whether she truly found peace in the end, and I recall the words on her memorial card, referring to Brenda as one who "accepted Christ at Chicago Uptown Ministry" very shortly before she died. When we talked over coffee and doughnuts, I asked her how she heard God, and how and where she found the time to listen. She could say exactly. "Like yesterday, when I was in church. The preacher was preaching, and I thought that was a sign of God trying to tell me to get my life back together. I believe him. God is the number one person in my life. I love him too, and without him I wouldn't be here on this earth."

When asked why she didn't just give up, she seemed just a little disappointed in me for asking. "I still have faith. I choose not to give up. I know [drugs and alcohol] is a sin. I don't have an answer for that yet. But I do know he's there. I feel close to God. Right now. Here." She speaks her truth: clearly, persuasively.

A couple of weeks later (and long before Brenda dies), Darla, Brenda's partner, is talking. Her mother had died of cocaine abuse and she was terrified of her drug-dealing father, yet she had steel in her sinews and faith in her daily life. Why? And what sustained her? She, too, knew exactly. "They say God ain't going to give you more than what you can handle. God has been there all the time. Even though I wasn't going to church, I would pray at home. My mother and her mother told me everything [about God]. He's the reason for my life. He's the reason for my breathing. He wakes me up every morning. And I know what I've got to do, and nothin's impossible."

Has she never been tempted to give up? She is adamant: "No! Because without God there'd be no air, nothing: no land. He created everything. I believe this. I talk to God. Every night I talk to God. I pray that he'll give me strength to make it another day, that he looks over my kids, and that all the people in my life now—that he gives me strength to deal with me. I can't describe what God looks like 'cause I've never seen him. But I can say I think God is caring, understanding, forgiving. I was raised like that, through my mother and grandmother. I know my grandmother believed wholeheartedly in "the man upstairs." That's what she said. She got it from the Bible. I've read the Bible. Not all the way through from beginning to end. But I have read a lot of psalms. A lot of things."

No doubt God is quite real for Darla, but that reality is not mediated by institutional religion, and her faith seems not to need it. Like many of the women, Darla seems able to manage quite well without Jesus. I ask her about this. My question is as irrelevant as unexpected. She struggles to respond. "Well, he was God's son. I guess [he's in my life]...I mean God gave us Jesus for our sins. But I still don't understand why he did that. I know people say Christmas is the birth of Jesus, but it don't register."

Can she say more about her experience of God through all her struggles? Relaxed now, she laughs wryly: "He's been there! In everything I've done. Everything I've succeeded in, he's helped me to do. He got my ID, my birth certificate...He does! He woke me up in order to give me the strength and energy to go look."

But where was God when she was raped, and why didn't God get her a job? Darla refuses to be drawn: "He did give me a job!" Then she goes quiet, thinking about the rape. "But...I don't know about that. Maybe I wasn't doing the right thing...I don't know. Sometimes I think maybe God puts you through bad things in order to get you to see other things. I never lose faith in God. Sometimes I let myself down, as well as other people. But it's not intentional all the time. Sometimes I do intend to let myself down. I make situations for myself that I can't get out of and I end up in deep trouble. Then I regret it later. But I never give up. Not on God, no! On life? Yeah. They are a lot different. I feel as though if I give up on life that's just saying 'I want to end life; I don't want to be on this earth anymore.' I've done that. God's not there then. Because then I'm not thinking about God, I'm thinking about me. I'm being selfish. Selfishness is me wanting to kill myself. But anything can bring God back into the picture. If someone says something nice to me, bam! I'm back! Like I've never been anywhere."

Selfishness is me wanting to kill myself, she said. *Our hearts are restless until they rest in God,* Augustine said. They both knew that lives will be destroyed unless people live with integrity. Darla has equally strong *pensées* on churchiness: "Church people? They say things, then they do the opposite. They go to church and praise God, but the next day....They say you shouldn't put impurities in your body or smoke cigarettes, but they are doing it themselves. I don't agree with that. Some of the ministers...some of them actually believe and practice what they preach. But some, I know, they don't. I guess they backslide, or whatever. I shouldn't have to go to a place to worship. I could be here, in the hallway. Because he [God] sees everything you do. He sees every step you take. He hears what you say. He sees what you do. And what you do to other people, he knows."

Many people say they do not need a formal place of worship in order to pray—but they rarely pray themselves. Darla does pray, and as far as she is concerned she does not need a church.

Ranita is a good person. She struggles with a huge inferiority complex, but she is committed to helping others and to persevering. Does God strengthen her indomitable spirit? As always, she is direct and candid. "God for me is...my intuition; something eating at me. My mom was pretty religious. A Baptist. She brought us up in the Church. I sang in the choir. After she died, I strayed away from Church. I haven't been back since, but I do pray. I don't understand the Bible. I did have a *Good News Bible*, but I'm still very confused about many things. I was going to do a Bible class...but it's like I have to start from the beginning. I'm lazy sometimes."

Ranita is consistent: having acknowledged her lazy streak, she does not blame God or indulge in self-pity when she considers her life to date. "God is real. He's real. He's blessing me a lot. I used to be angry with God because I used to see a lot of people around me with many material blessings. I never knew how to recognize my own blessings. One thing I came to recognize is the blessing of my health. I suffer high blood pressure and obesity. But basically that's all the blessing I need: my health. I know material things are not that important."

When asked about Jesus, about Church, her frustration and peevishness intrude:

"Jesus? Basically…I don't have a term or definition for Jesus. It's as if the Spirit moves within me. God is real. Jesus is the Son of God, but it's not as if he's the same. I do use the name Jesus because that's the name given to me. Christmas, as I get older, it doesn't mean the same. As a God thing? No….The Church? Church people to me are hypocrites and phony—although I would love to go back and sing in a choir. I really want that. That's what I'm going to strive for. I went to [pastor] Coleman's church and really enjoyed her teachings. She is so positive. I'm trying to learn how to be positive. My negative thinking surfaces all the time. Church people are the main ones that talk about you. You try to follow in their footsteps, and they are doing something like talking about the next person. Church itself is OK. I know a church where they say you can wear pants. I haven't wore a skirt or dress since I don't know when. Because I'm obese and my thighs rub together when I wear a dress…"

Lynette, addicted early to crack, and prolific mother of children whose names all begin, like hers, with "L," surely has plenty of reasons to be angry: even, perhaps particularly, at God. Astoundingly, she remains positive: "I do believe there is a God. He worked a miracle in my life. It could not have happened unless there was some kind of spiritual presence. As far as getting me into this mess in the first place, that was not God. No, no, no: that was the devil, right there. Not God. I pray to God all the time. I might be sitting, standing, kneeling. I ask for strength, humility…. I got this from my grandparents, and I know my children have it. They went to church…I go to church. Baptist. I wasn't religious when I was doing drugs, but now I am. Before, yes; after, yes. It makes a whole lot of difference. Being on that spiritual level helps me maintain my daily life and realize there is a bigger spiritual presence than myself. My mother's parents told me. I guess I've always believed it. I go to Rev. Johnston's church here in Uptown. The ladies from the shelter go, all the time. He is very open and spiritual. He talks to us and asks us different questions to think and talk about. There are about twenty people involved."

Next is Lisa, whose life is littered with a series of near-collapses. She explains very well, what keeps her alive and able to live positively. "I used to go to sleep drinking and wake up drinking. You gotta have willpower. I got it now. From God. God goes all the way back with me, as far as I remember, to the age of five. My mom used to take us to the Baptist church all the time. I stopped going at age eighteen. I don't know why. I like it when I was a kid. Now God is part of my life. I know in my heart, all the things I ain't done. I don't know how to say it: but I'm only human. They [God] is one—Jesus, God, and the Holy Spirit. I pray to all of them. I pray in the name of Jesus. I call on him. I don't know what I think of…an old man…if I say 'in the name of Jesus' who am I praying to? I ain't been to church recently." Theologian she may not be: church member she is not. But person of faith she most certainly is.

Janet, adopted and abused, was introduced to religion by her parents but found God on her own. "My mom was a Mormon— can you imagine that!—and I joined the Mormon church. She took me. They were strict. Cliquish. I didn't like it too much. I didn't go too often. My adopted friend went to an Episcopal church. I never really learned anything there. I'm not particularly religious. I believe in God. God created us; that's why we are here. Creator of all things. That kind of stuff. I would say God is part of my life. I pray a lot. I pray that I get out of here soon, and that my friends will be all right. And to help my friends out. I try to pray for other people, not just myself. I believe in it. It's useful."

"Jesus is God's Son. I pray to both of them, I guess. And they're both the same. It's hard to explain. But when I pray, it's to God. I know some of the story of Jesus. From the Mormons. He is our Savior. I *would* like to know more. Christmas and Easter are important to me. I'm usually alone. But they are very important. They are separate from my life and concerns about survival."

Deborah is mentally unstable, not helped by her early life and her mother's perfidy. With such a fragile self-image, she might be a candidate for suicide or murder. But Deborah clings to faith, finds meaning in her life, and has reason to hope. Amazingly.

"My brothers and sisters don't help much. My mom would read the Bible every day. We went to the Baptist church every week. Now I go to church here. I like to go, basically, to get spiritual help. I go and get prayed for by the pastor. He knows me. I pray before I go to sleep every night. I pray for my life. God, for me, is someone you pray to if you want to live a good life and be prosperous. Jesus is close...to everybody. I think about the miracles he has been doing in the Bible. I pray to the God who created everything. But Jesus is important to me. They are both the same to me."

The fact that the pastor knows her is evidently a critical reason that keeps her coming to the church. It is not the Bible study or the liturgy, or even the preaching that Deborah values, but the personal contact. She feels the pastor knows her. This is inner knowledge; it creates a relationship. She is not simply a member of his church or a nameless recipient of his ministry.

It was Janice who told me about Brenda's brutal murder. She knows violence firsthand: her own brother was murdered. But she had said, "I can't complain," and I wondered why not. "God is in my life a whole lot. Yes! Even though I don't go to church like I should, but lately I've been going a lot more. I feel I have him all in my heart. I get up in the morning and I'm thankful, and I think [of that] throughout the day. Before I go to bed, I say my prayers. I try to put him first, and not me. I thank God for letting me wake up in the morning. That's good!"

Janice is very enthusiastic now. But does she blame God for anything? Like others, she is almost shocked at the question. "Blame God? I never blamed God for anything. I just never thought of that. I started coming closer to God as I got closer to forty. I do my prayers privately a lot. But I'm starting to go to church again. I would say God is close, yes. God is...peaceful...caring."

Does she think about Jesus? She hesitates. "I guess, not Jesus. I don't think about anything Jesus did or said. I have heard about that, but that's about it. When I think about God I believe it's a peaceful place where everyone gets along, there is no violence …God is just like heaven. God is in everybody. I think of God as a nice peaceful place I like to be."

Janice is the least specific of all the women. But clearly God has a place in her life. Clearly her life makes a place for God. This is endlessly fascinating…

Lorraine was raised Greek Orthodox. Knowing that she became homeless only in her seventies, I wonder what that experience did to her faith. Is God still part of her life? "Yes. Since I was a child I have always prayed every night. I believe it will really help you. I pray that my children are healthy and the boys have a good life and…the way drugs are today; they are heavy on the street…. I pray for myself too. Yes. For courage and strength. God does hear. I know he's always around and will help. He is like a spirit, a shadow. I go to the Baptist church a lot. I like that church. I like the preachers a lot. I stayed four and a half hours once! The preacher could really talk and explain! I took a girl with me once. She said she didn't believe in God. But a few weeks later she went again, by herself!

"Jesus is a holy spirit and he helps people who believe in him. I usually pray to God. Jesus is important, too. He is the Son. I'm close to God. Jesus is a holy man, a very religious person.

"I don't blame God! It's not God's fault. It's the city's fault. I don't feel sorry for myself. I just feel strong."

Twelve women, twelve stories; but so many resonances, so many common themes, experiences, and convictions. Listening to the individual stories and reflecting on their cumulative effect provides ample food for contemplation, and many suggestions—implicit and explicit—of how Christian ministry could be brought more in line with the ministry of Jesus and with the needs, not to say the rights, of God's poor.

PART II

An Outsider History of Homelessness: Theological and Pastoral Reflections

14

HOMELESS WOMEN AND POPULAR PIETY[1]

> Evangelization loses much of its force if it does not take into consideration the actual people to whom it is addressed, if it does not use their language, their signs and symbols, if it does not answer the questions they ask, and if it does not have an impact on their concrete life.[2]
>
> POPE PAUL VI, *EVANGELII NUNTIANDI*, 1975

A much more recent Roman document[3] includes many references to the concreteness and actuality of culture, stating that "culture is the whole of human activity, human intelligence and emotions, the human quest for meaning, human customs and ethics" (PCC, 2), and asserting that "the pastoral approach to culture focuses on real situations..." (PCC, 6). It identifies the "huge agglomerations of people who are socially rootless, politically powerless, economically marginalized and culturally isolated," and "people whose lives are unraveled" (PCC, 8).

Focusing on culture and people, the document makes three interrelated points. First: "The church asserts the dignity of the human person...and affirming her preferential option for the poor and excluded, the church is duty bound to promote a culture of

solidarity at every level of society" (*PCC*, 21). Second: "If...
pastoral workers, Christian communities and qualified theologians...are to touch people's hearts, [then] proclaiming the
Gospel...and celebrating salvation in the liturgy demand not only
a profound knowledge of the faith but also a knowledge of the
cultural environment" (*PCC*, 27). Third: "Popular piety is the
way a people expresses its faith and its relationship to God and
[God's] Providence... (*PCC*, 28).

These noble sentiments and admirable instructions are not
new, even though many (pastoral workers, Christian communities, and qualified theologians) may have failed to hear or practice them. Yet sadly, this document fails to pursue the implications of its own statements. After the impressive rhetoric, we might
not notice the assumption on which the remainder of the text
appears to rest: that "culture" applies only to a homogeneous,
stable, or dominant social reality. The document simply overlooks
some of the most brute social facts of our times, and a highly
significant minority of the population: homeless people.

Let us sketch the features of a social reality that cries out for
a deeper and more informed pastoral outreach. The churches,
through their institutional structure or individual or community
responses, are pivotal in responding to the needs of poor and
needy people. Yet typically, such outreach is not understood as
legitimate "evangelization"; clergy and other professional ministers are not prominently involved; and though some homeless
people attend church, a significant number deliberately avoid the
"high" churches (particularly Roman Catholic), preferring the
"low" (particularly Baptist). The outreach advocated here, therefore, would take Paul VI's sentiments very seriously, as well as the
even more pointed words of Jesus himself. Jesus articulates a kind
of job description for himself (and for his followers: Matthew
25:35ff), when he declares: "The Spirit of the Lord is upon me"—
and then identifies the poor, captives, the blind and oppressed,
the rootless, disenfranchised pariahs, as the beneficiaries of his
Spirit-led, healing, restoring, humanizing ministry (Luke 4:18).

SOCIAL FACTS

The twentieth century saw human degradation and destabilization on an unprecedented scale, yet the torrid pace is being maintained in the twenty-first. Refugees, asylum seekers, and displaced people are among the most visible; but the growing numbers of urban poor have been perhaps the least visible. If the plight of the visible (in Kosovo, Sierra Leone, Afghanistan, Iraq, Sudan or Palestine/Israel) provokes a humanitarian response, the plight of many on our own doorstep has simply not been noticed.

A profile of the homeless poor provides a context for thoughts about popular religiosity and pastoral responses. Homelessness and poverty are inextricably linked. As Jesus ruefully said, "You always have the poor with you" (Matthew 26:11). Indeed, those whom Jesus encountered in first-century Palestine are with us in the twenty-first-century United States, especially in the faces of homeless people: mostly nocturnal, largely invisible, easily avoidable and virtually uncountable, because they are an unstable and shifting population. It is easier to identify trends than to produce incontestable statistics: mere facts do not convince everyone. "The homeless poor" is more than a category; it is fragile culture of flesh and blood people. And Jesus gave them preferential treatment.

In 1997, 35.6 million Americans (13.3 percent of the population) lived in poverty; 41 percent of these (14.6 million) had incomes *less than half the poverty level*.[4] That year alone, 675,000 people lost health insurance due to welfare reform legislation. In the twenty years after 1973, 2.25 million low-rent units disappeared, while between 1991 and 1995, low-income rents rose 21 percent. By 1995 the number of low-income renters outstripped available units by 4.4 million. Add the casualties of domestic violence, mental illness, and addiction disorders, and the cohort of homeless people in this country is as populous as a small nation. In every city, official estimates of the homeless population exceed the available bed space, and rural areas are relatively worse than urban centers. Homelessness results, largely, from people being forced to choose between (because they cannot afford all) food, shelter, and other basic needs.

An infra-red "snapshot" of the United States taken on a balmy spring night (winter is much worse) would show around 700 thousand men, women and children *in officially designated shelters*, and up to two million more "hidden homeless" sleeping in the open or in abandoned cars or buildings. But perhaps 12 million Americans have been homeless at some time, and more than half (6.6 million) experienced homelessness in the past five years. On average, every cot in a shelter accommodates between four and six people per year; and between 1987 and 1997 shelter capacity increased by almost 300 percent. It would be bad enough if these were statistics; tragically, the figures represent real people. To our shame, many of us fail to notice.

REAL PEOPLE

How do people survive the dislocation and trauma of homelessness? How do they find or maintain some vestige of meaning for their lives? Why do so many manage to cling to their dignity, humor, and faith, when their daily round is so undignified and the promises of organized religion are so hollow? Where is "The Church"— committed Christians, pastoral programs, and honest outreach?

By description more than an analysis; in pastoral rather than sociological terms; and as an attempt to identify the "inner history," the following remarks apply specifically to a scattered group of people, constantly changing but countable in the hundreds of thousands on any given night: the homeless women of America.

As the brute statistics indicate, homeless people are grouped in many categories, to be transformed into stereotypes or social stigmas: mentally defectives; substance abusers; socially unskilled; unemployable; claustrophobic; feckless; losers. Such are the labels affixed to human persons with inner lives; in fact their inner lives are often their most important identifier and the most convincing explanation of their survival. So why are these inner lives so little explored, belittled, or misunderstood by the Christian community? A glimpse into the lives of the homeless poor reveals extremely interesting manifestations of popular religiosity, a form of noninstitutional Christianity that points an accusing finger at the churches and congregations which overlook these people and their plight.[5]

POPULAR RELIGION

"Popular religiosity" has a condescending ring, and "popular religion" is not much better, because the connotations of "popular" and "religiosity" separate it from mainstream experience and approval.[6] "The religion of (the) people" or "(ordinary) people's religion" may be an improvement, if one intends to identify people's honest—and therefore authentic—attempts to communicate in a godly manner both with God and humanity. By whatever name, popular religion is largely informal (unformalized), not organized (unorganized), and at variance with the declared orthodoxy of a particular institutional church.

Such religious expression represents the honest efforts of those separated from institutional religion, due to excommunication, feelings of worthlessness, a sense of personal unacceptability, lack of evangelization, or the perceived irrelevance of organized and formal religion.[7] As Pope Paul VI said, unless evangelization is addressed to real people in their concrete situations it loses much of its force—precisely why orthodox religion loses many adherents. Many homeless people have a profound desire to worship, but either feel excluded by mainstream Christianity, or are simply unable to identify with its doctrinaire approach or with what they perceive as middle-class membership and hypocrisy.

Popular religiosity is alive and well in our cities. It is "popular" in three senses: "regarded with favor or approval"; "pertaining to or representing the common people"; and "of the people as a whole—the general masses." To many middle-class people, such dictionary definitions imply vulgarity, and certainly otherness. Such "popularity" has no social cachet. To many upwardly mobile Christians, imbued with the Protestant (work) Ethic, it is not only alien but reprehensible. The official Church, wittingly or not, is tarred with the same brush.

The "inner history" of a person or a people represents their own perspective as they experience a particular, concrete, bounded world. Many of us know some "outer history": we know *about* other people or their worlds. But such knowledge can be obtained in the comfort of an armchair or a desk. In order to comprehend people's "inner history," we must encounter them.

Jesus knew much more than people's outer history; he *actually knew real persons: this* rich young man, *that* tax collector, *this* women caught in adultery, *that* centurion, and so on. In encountering them, he responded to their existential situation, whether they were named (Bartimaeus or Nicodemus, Mary or Martha), or anonymous (the widow, the woman who poured ointment, or the other women: the Syrophoenician or the Samaritan).

It is pastorally unacceptable merely to *know about* people, or cultures: Jesus calls for authentic encounters. One shortcoming of "Toward a Pastoral Approach to Culture" is its very title: you cannot approach "culture": any honest pastoral approach must be to actual people. The homeless poor are people before they are statistics or components of culture.

OFFICIAL RELIGION

Sketching the broad lines of popular and official religion, and comparing practices and practitioners, is only a beginning: it may help us to *know about*. A step toward *actually knowing* people identified with popular religion would be to ask: why might they respond in this (unofficial) way, and not in other (official) ways? More pointedly, how does "popular religion" describe what its devotees experience as popular, congenial, attractive, and relevant to their actual lives? Seven categories may help.[8]

FIGURE 1: Categories of Popular and Official Religion

Categories	Popular Religion	Official Religion
Thought Structure	*Principle of Participation:* Everything is related and interdependent. Belief is informal or unformalized.	*Principle of Contradiction:* Every thing and person is discrete and different. Belief is codified and formalized.
The Sacred	Sacred and profane distinguishable and distinguished, but not dichotomized. Utilitarian considerations (orthopraxy) govern religious action.	Religious faith and expression are often perceived as sacred, and distinct from ordinary life. Doctrine (orthodoxy) governs religious action.
Nature and The World	Nature itself is to be respected; it is holy. All creation is interrelated, both animate and inanimate.	Nature is profane and minimally integrated with religious action. It is used, exploited, and dominated.[9]
Space and Time	There are special places and times, but *all* is permeated by the holy or sacred. *Ritualization* celebrates the holy.	Only official times and places are sacred. *Consecration* makes things/persons holy.
Social Politics	Popular religion (religiosity) is rooted in marginalization and oppression; it is always different from official religion.	Official religion is for and of the centers of privilege and respectability; popular religion is abnormal.
Historical Project	It looks to a better future for the poor; it implies radical social change.	It accepts the progressive evolution of human history; God legitimizes human achievements and possessions.
Social Organization	"Horizontal" rather than "vertical" relationships are important; people are united by their common experiences.	Structures are perceived as "vertical" and hierarchically ordered; people are separated by their differing statuses.

No social model is perfect or watertight. But models can help us understand the broad contours of worlds of experience and fields of relationships, so as to extrapolate from and compare the "inner history" of different people. As far as homeless persons are concerned, this model needs some fine-tuning. But it might provide a point of entry into other worlds of meaning.

The world and culture of homeless people are *different* from that of salary-earning, job-secure, educated, insured homeowners, even though these worlds touch and sometimes overlap. Homeless people must discover or create meaning, for the conventional meanings of the dominant culture do not translate very well. Unless they engage meaningfully with others, they will go mad or perish. But homeless people are ingenious and hopeful. It is said that after a natural disaster or nuclear catastrophe, the homeless poor would be among the least traumatized and the first to survive. But their survival would be attributable as much to their solidarity and cooperation (their shared meanings and symbols: their culture) as to individual initiative.

People's Religion

Generally, homeless people's belief(s) or convictions are neither formalized nor standardized, and many such people synthesize elements that others would find logically incompatible. Thus they may cling to an all-loving God, despite their experience of an unjust and capricious world; God will always be there, even though "there" is an abandoned car or condemned building. Oscar Wilde quipped that "we are all in the gutter, but some of us are looking at the stars"; but the needs of those actually in the gutter but unable to see the stars are different from stargazers. Like frightened animals in a headlamp's glare, some homeless people are petrified or destroyed. Yet many have histories—and *her-stories*—which, given time, they love to share with more "conventional" people with a more "official" religious perspective. Their antisocial or unsocialized behaviors may yield to graciousness, wit and wisdom. Given time (rare enough: though they may be given hand-outs, or "services"), they are perfectly able to reciprocate. Yet it may take years to establish trust on the ruins of lives that have suffered the abuse of people in general and men in particular, and institutions in general and the churches in particular.

Popular religion is unorthodox but not entirely privatized. Among homeless people it is an expression of interiority, not to say withdrawal. But it is also social: many homeless women do go to church (or churches) alone or with others, rarely or often. They are not typical "smorgasbord Christians": they are not looking, how-ever unconsciously, for an easy life, but for meaning, survival, and an injection of hope. Their starting point, almost literally, is the gutter. But their hope is survival and their survival is their hope.

COMMUNION OF SAINTS

The communion of saints comprises all living persons of truth and love. Divine blessing cannot be limited [to the Church]. *Within human cultures everywhere* the Spirit calls persons to *seek truth and live in love and justice with others*, so that "friends of God and prophets" can be found in every tongue and nation, even among religion's cultured despisers.[10]

The words are Beth Johnson's; the emphasis is mine. We might even add to the final phrase, "…and among the despised, forgot-ten, or overlooked faithful." Perhaps we can elaborate on these thoughts, and extend their implicit reach to cover the homeless poor more explicitly.

The Spirit calls the communion of saints from "within hu-man cultures." Many people do not consider the homeless popu-lation as part of culture, but to deny culture to homeless people is to victimize them doubly! By including "all living persons of faith and love," Johnson's definition certainly allows homeless people to qualify! But that raises another question: if the communion of saints does include homeless people, what are the implications for the rest of us?

If, as Johnson argues, the communion of saints is not only a helpful theological notion but a description of people of faith, it follows that Christian ministry should acknowledge and respond to the needs of all whose faith is fiercely strong, whose hope springs eternal, but whose religion is either invisible or unorthodox. The major issue here, then, is not just about how we open our doors to the lost and the strayed, but about how, and when, and where we actually go forth into the "highways and byways," to encounter, embrace, and offer healing and hospitality, as Jesus did.

POPULAR PIETY

Where *is* the religion of people (popular religion) when not expressed in official, orthodox forms and in churches and canonical parishes? What is the challenge to ministers with a missionary heart? Here are the words of women of faith who are currently homeless in the United States. Here is their piety, from their perspective, from their "inner history." Here is search for the transcendent, indomitable hope, tolerance and altruism. Something very godly is palpably part of their lives. Paul VI told us to pay attention to *actual people, the questions they ask*, and the impact of the Gospel on *their concrete life*. Here then, are half a dozen personal testimonies.[11] [Fuller versions are in chapter 13.]

> "God's been holding me up. He's been real good to me, keeping me where I can keep the faith, and away from drugs and alcohol....I read the Bible a lot....A lot of church people have done things I don't think church people should do or even think. That would not make me confide in them....I got angry at God and I did used to blame God for my life. But I'm not against God. My faith is growing stronger. I got hope. I do Bible study twice a week. We take a passage and discuss it" (Tina).

"I believe in God, I do. I pray every night before [bed-time]. If I do good or bad, I pray for another day. Every day I wake up I thank God for another day....Blame God? Why? I can't blame God.... I have abandoned the church many times, but I need God in my life" (Jeanette).

"I cried for two days. It's really scary. But I had my faith. I believe in God very seriously. God kept me going. I just prayed and talked to God every day. There were times I wanted to give up, but God had business....I read the Bible....I want to die a happy death, and I know I'm going to live forever in paradise" (Lunette).

"I been baptized five or six times, because I'm a back-slider. I pray to God. God is in my heart. I believe in the Lord. But yesterday was the first time I've been in church for ten years. I do think that God loves me. I know God works in mysterious ways. He's there for me; I still have faith; I choose not to give up" (Brenda).

"God's been there all the time, even though I wasn't going to church. I would pray at home. God is the reason for my life. Nothin's impossible....I can't describe God, but I think he's caring, understanding, forgiving. I've read the Bible....God's always there, in everything I've done. He's helped me. He woke me up to give me strength and energy to go look for [ID and documents]. I never give up on God, no!... I'd go to church if someone went with me. I wouldn't go by myself....Church people: they say things, then they do the opposite. I never went to church for help or assistance. I shouldn't have to go [to a special place] to worship" (Darla).

"God is…my intuition; something eating at me. After my mom died, I strayed from the church.…I don't understand the Bible.…God is real! He's blessing me a lot. I used to be angry with God because I saw many people with material blessings.…Jesus? I don't have a term or definition for Jesus. It's as if the Spirit moves within me. God is real. Jesus is the son of God, but it's not as if he's the same.…The Church? Church people to me are hypocrites and phony. I would like to try a church; church itself is OK" (Ranita).

Conclusion

Jesus said to his disciples, "ask, seek, knock" (see Matthew 7:7–8). He embellishes this, later, promising that whatever his disciples ask for in his name will be granted (John 16:23–24, 26). But people with all the answers do not stop to ask; those who say they are not lost, refuse to seek; those secure within their own comfortable domain do not need to knock. These three commands apply to inquirers, searchers, outsiders. An institution that has all the answers, is convinced it has reached its goal, and occupies the center will tend at best to invite others to the center but not to consider moving to the margins. But the homeless poor actually live at the margins and either fail to hear or to be convinced by general invitations to gather at the center. So they continue to struggle, to fashion a world of meaning in the face of chaos and confusion, and to eke out their existence on the very edges (and beyond) of the institutional church.

It is always time for a new evangelization, but not didactic or threatening proselytism. It must begin by seeking invisible and excluded persons, not in order to baptize but to serve, by learning their inner history and by treating them as Jesus would—and did.

15

PRACTICING COLLABORATIVE MINISTRY[1]

To some people, *collaborative ministry* suggests compromise, watering the truth, or a dereliction of duty. They think ministry is the exercise of authority which should not be compromised by collaboration—with "separated brethren," people of other faiths or none, NGOs, or "ordinary people." Yet collaborative ministry is at the heart of the life of Jesus.

Ministry is found most characteristically in modest service. Jesus was first and foremost a *minister* or servant, the opposite of a *magister* or master. His followers were warned not to be like ostentatious Pharisees who accepted such titles as *rabbi* or *master* (Matthew 23:8). They must undertake small, apparently insignificant (yet often important) tasks. Masters pursue more grandiose (apparently significant) undertakings.

Collaboration is found in the one who chose twelve rather limited individuals, though willing assistants, to work with him in a special way (Mark 3:13–14; Matthew 6:7); who commissioned and sent the seventy(-two)—themselves working collaboratively in dyads—into all the villages he intended to visit

(Luke 10:1); and who issued the poignant invitation: "Come to me, all you who labor *and are burdened*, and I will give you rest. *Take my yoke upon you and learn from me*" (Matthew 11:28, italics mine). That's collaboration.

Practical Theology

To some people, *practical theology* sounds like an oxymoron. Such people think of theology as a deductive process whose conclusions follow inevitably from incontestable premises, and not something to be constructed from context or consensus. This view of theology has a long pedigree.

Christians with a true missionary spirit have always aspired to practice what Jesus preached: an incarnated, apostolic spirituality that engages with and learns from the people. This brings theology down to earth, as Jesus did. His words are the litmus test: are we responding to the cry of the poor, the pleas of the needy, the hopes of the oppressed—or pursuing an agenda that makes us feel virtuous but fails to read the signs of the times? *Practical theology* is grounded in *praxis*, moves from there to *theory*, and then returns, renewed, to *praxis*.

The first "moment" is *praxis:* more than *practice* or routine activity, it is *the application of knowledge and skills, experience and wisdom, accumulated by exposure to reality.* Christians who are truly *confirmed* in their baptism, seek such ministry, and their lives generate abundant pastoral experience: they go "looking for trouble," with the explicit intention of doing something to alleviate it. Mature reflection on such experience leads to the second "moment": encounter with theory.

However rich our experience, we must not be seduced by activism. Socrates was right: the unexamined life is not worth living. We are all called to absorb and apply a missionary or missional theology (the gauge of genuine Christianity). The understanding and *praxis* of mission have developed enormously in recent years. Contemporary missiological insights can prepare us for the final "moment," which returns us to *praxis*. But our perspectives will be different: we will be refocused and recommitted to the One who calls and sends. Practical theology can change lives.

FORMATIVE EXPERIENCE: PRAXIS

Collaborative *ministry* is a necessary counterbalance to *magistry*, and perhaps the only valid approach to mission. It is necessary if a balance is to be maintained between leadership and service, between the ordinary and extraordinary aspects of life. Practical theology helps us maintain a balance between the extremes of activism and speculation. But first, an example of a formative experience: *praxis*.

Rosalee is conventionally classed as mentally handicapped ("challenged" is the contemporary term), but one night at the shelter she was the challenger rather than the challenged. Like many deprived, invisible, and "insignificant" members of society, she was direct and unafraid, and she spoke truth. Like many privileged, visible, and "significant" members of society, I was quite unprepared for her message. She radically undermined my approach to ministry.

As I was serving nourishing, well-cooked food, I sensed rather than saw Rosalee approaching, her head moving sideways, her face a mixture of sadness and reproach. "You know the trouble with you, Tony?" she intoned—without preamble and evidently intending to give me the answer. "You never ask us what *we* want to eat." I stopped in mid-serving, words of self-justification and rebuke already forming: *How dare she? She should be glad of a good meal!* But even as the thought took shape, I knew she was right: *I* was the giver, the initiative-taker, in control. *I* decided what everyone should eat, what was good for them. And *I* expected them to be uncomplaining and grateful!

Rosalee knew that I had not included the women in the plans for their own well-being. Of course they were grateful for a hot meal! Nevertheless, they would like to have been asked their likes and dislikes, she said. Of course they would accept whatever they were given! But still, they would like to be included in the equation, she said. Then she stopped.

Very tentatively then, I asked Rosalee what the women would like the following week. "If you *do* ask us, we'll just tell you to bring what you always bring," she said. "But then we have helped to choose it, then you will know that we want to eat it as much as you want to cook it!" *Praxis* is the absorption of and reflection on experience, done in such a way that it brings about a *new* response. It is sometimes painful but always necessary. Rosalee was the catalyst that night.

Yet a response alone is insufficient. Experience must engage with some kind of theory—a coherent set of principles or methods—lest the response be ill judged.

From Praxis to Theory

Rosalee can represent the myriad people we claim to serve one way or another. She is a subject and not merely an object of our good will and commitment. Like the mother of Jesus, watching amazing events in her life (Luke 2:19), we whose faith-filled ministry leads us to our own Rosalees, have the obligation to "treasure all these things, [...] ponder them in [our] hearts," and apply what we learn.

The Church has a rich history of cross-cultural ministry, both intercontinental and closer to home, across divides of ethnicity, social class, religious identity, or civil society. Every serious-minded Christian accumulates experience and skills (*praxis*) that can be brought into dialogue with contemporary mission theology (*theory*) to produce a renewed and reinvigorated missionary response (*praxis*). For years we have said the primary agents of inculturation[2] are the Holy Spirit and the local people. Have we overlooked the wisdom in that insight and claimed and clung to a dominant role? God is in charge. Our responsibility is to reflect on the unfolding experience of our lives and respond again and again to the Spirit who blows where the Spirit wills, and not only or always where we happen to be.

Unless we are accountable for our *praxis* and judged against the Church's *developing* understanding of the implications of mission (a *process* that our own *praxis* may actually help to shape), we may end up taking initiatives that are not ours, unintentionally "doing our own thing," and acting quite inappropriately.

How should we act? We may need an attitudinal shift. John Paul II strongly encouraged those engaged in mission to attend to context and consensus, and urged collaboration with the people they serve, and immersion in their lives, languages and cultures. They must "mov[e] beyond their own cultural limitations" (*Redemptoris Missio*, 52, 53). But more is required: deep reflection on the demands of mission in the contemporary world is imperative.

HALF A CENTURY OF MISSIOLOGY

"The Church has a mission": this was axiomatic in classical mission theology. But hidden structural faults in that theology slowly became apparent: both "church" and "mission" were in urgent need of attention.

According to *Mystici Corporis* (22, 103) of Pius XII, "The Church" is the Roman Catholic Church alone. The only hope of salvation for *all* others was through some kind of "Baptism of desire" for the One, True Church. This theological high-handedness legitimated some Catholic attitudes that were very unchristian. We can surely sympathize with the reaction of Christian missionaries of other denominations who endured the Roman Catholic Church's claim to be the initiator and arbiter of mission, and ultimate destiny of all humanity. All Christians understood mission as the means by which the Church encountered the world in order to bring it into conformity with Christ—but everyone had different ideas of Church, and of what such conformity entailed.

In a landmark elaboration of "Church," Vatican II went far beyond Pius XII. *Lumen Gentium* speaks now of the unique Church of Christ which we profess to be one, holy, catholic and apostolic....This Church, constituted and organized as a society in the present world, *subsists in the Catholic Church,* which is governed by the successor of Peter and the bishops in communion with him. Nevertheless, many elements of sanctification and of truth are found outside its visible confines (*LG,* 8).

This represented a potential breakthrough in ecumenical relations, but much more was ahead: *Unitatis Redintegratio* acknowledged that other churches have no need for an unconscious desire to belong to the Catholic Church; that the gifts of the Spirit are shared by all Christian churches; and that the "separated churches" are truly Church (*UR,* 13–24). The implications for ecumenical collaboration became increasingly apparent in the following years.[3]

Before the Council, however, Catholic mission theology presented a Church-centered and Church-focused view of mission, identifying the twin missionary motivations as the salvation of souls and the planting of the (Roman Catholic) Church. As long as mission was chained to the Church, and the Church was given priority over mission, there would be little development in mission theology. Hindsight shows that four themes were slowly developing. They broke through at Vatican II, and their lasting impact changed the face of missiology.

Mission Is God's Business

Long before the Council, the prevailing grandiose missiology was beginning to be challenged—ironically perhaps, by Protestants. The change came through the rediscovery of the significance of *Missio Dei*—God's mission or "involvement in and with the world."[4] The (Protestant) International Missionary Council was emphasizing that God is the initiator of mission. By 1952 there had been an "almost imperceptible shift from a Church-centered mission to a mission-centered Church."[5] Now the implications became clearer: God's creative enterprise is prior both to the Church and to its mission. The word *mission* belongs properly to God. Indeed it could almost stand as a description of God: outreaching, ingathering, healing, reconciling, and transforming all humanity.

To the image of the Father sending the Son and both sending the Spirit was added the notion of the Trinity itself commissioning the Church and imparting to it a centrifugal momentum. Now we could speak almost routinely, not of the Church having a mission but of the mission having a Church. The Church exists for mission, or as *Ad Gentes* puts it, the Church on earth is by its very nature missionary since, according to the plan of the Father, it has its origin in the mission of the Son and the holy Spirit (*AG*, 2). This has enormous implications, not only for overseas mission but for every committed Christian.

The text then refers the opening paragraph of the *Lumen Gentium*, which contains a second important missiological insight: the Church as God's sign.

The Church as God's Sign

"The Church is a sacrament—a sign and instrument, that is, of communion with God and of the unity of the entire human race" (*LG*, 1). This identifies the Church as an agent (instrument) of human salvation, as well as a pointer (sign) of the relationship between God and humanity. The Church "will receive its perfection only in heaven," but has nevertheless been instituted by the Risen Christ as the "universal sacrament of salvation" (*LG*, 48); if the document were faithful to its patristic sources, *sacrament* would be understood as *sign* and *communion,* even more than as *agent* or *instrument.*[6] The implications were developed later, as the missionary aim of Christianizing the world was rethought, with profound effects on interreligious dialogue and collaborative ministry—at home no less than abroad. As the rethinking took place, a third profound insight was emerging: the Church is not the kingdom.

The Church Is Not the Kingdom

If the Church is understood *sacramentally* rather than *instrumentally*, its position in the world is relativized[7] and it is more readily differentiated from the kingdom (realm) of God. Jesus called people to repent before the imminent coming of the "kingdom of heaven" which was already-and-not-yet (Luke 11:20; 17:21; Matthew 3:2; 4:17). After the Resurrection he imparted his Spirit to the disciples, and "henceforward the church...receives the mission of proclaiming and establishing among all peoples *the kingdom* of Christ and of God, and is, on earth, the seed and the beginning of that kingdom" (*LG*, 5). This links, but does not merge, Church and kingdom: important in view of the next quarter century with its bold new initiatives like liberation theology which endeavored to apply this embryonic insight. The closest Vatican II came to pursuing it is in an allusion at the end of the *Gaudium et Spes:* "Here on earth the kingdom is mysteriously present; when the Lord comes it will enter into its perfection" (*GS*, 39).

In a careful presentation (but one lacking nuance) Pope John Paul II declared that attempts to proclaim the kingdom without simultaneously proclaiming the Church were unacceptable (*RM*, 18, 44): if missiology had been too ecclesiocentric before, it has now become too anthropocentric, too "focused on man's earthly needs" so that the kingdom becomes "something completely human and secularized" (*RM*, 17). The encyclical makes several pertinent points. First, the kingdom cannot be detached from Christ or from the Church; and the Church, while remaining distinct from both Christ and the kingdom, is indissolubly linked to both (*RM*, 18). Second, "the Church serves the Kingdom by establishing communities and founding new particular churches"; ...and "by spreading throughout the world *Gospel values* which are an expression of the Kingdom" (*RM*, 20). Third, "the inchoate reality of the Kingdom can also be found beyond the confines of the Church among peoples everywhere" (*RM*, 20).

The relationship between Church and kingdom remains the

center of current missiological concern. One of the great benefits of the debate is that mission can never be reduced to proclaiming heaven as a pot of spiritual gold at the end of the eschatological rainbow; nor can God be reduced to a *deus ex machina* trundled out at the end of time to distract attention from the injustice that abounds today. Which raises a fourth point: mission calls us to dialogue and discernment.

Mission Calls to Dialogue and Discernment

Two paragraphs in the only document (*Gaudium et Spes*) foreseen and intended by Pope John XXIII, articulate beautifully the importance of collaborative ministry as mission, and demonstrate that authentic missionary activity can be everywhere. They assert the wish of the Council—and by implication, of the members of the Church,

> to enter into dialogue with [humanity] about all the various problems [of the modern world], throwing the light of the Gospel on them and supplying humanity with the saving resources which the church has received from [Jesus]. It is the human person that is to be saved, human society which must be renewed. It is the human person, therefore, which is the key to this discussion, each individual human person in her or his totality, body and soul, heart and conscience, mind and will. This is why this holy synod...offers the whole human race the sincere cooperation of the church. [...] In every age, the church carries the responsibility of reading the signs of the times and of interpreting them in the light of the Gospel (*GS*, 3–4).

Our ministry may not call all of us to people like Rosalee, but we are *always* called to engage in appropriate ministry—*collaborative ministry*—not simply *for* the poor or *to* the needy, but *with* those whose lives may be changed by the encounter. And that, of course, must include ourselves. Unless *mission in reverse* (which seeks total conversion of the evangelizer) is deliberately undertaken, our best efforts will be undermined because our own conversion is not part of our missionary motivation. Our exposure to God's transforming grace is necessary, as Saint Paul reflects, "lest after preaching to others, I myself should be disqualified" (1 Corinthians 9:27).

That final phrase of *Gaudium et Spes* was a *leitmotif* of the pontificate of John XXIII and a hallmark of his authenticity. It was he who held the Church responsible for "reading the signs of the times"; Vatican II added the responsibility of "interpreting them in the light of the Gospel." But this hermeneutical skill is demanded as much of those who minister on the margins of megacities, as of those who are called overseas.

WHOSE BUSINESS IS IT?

Mission is the proper domain, the initiative, and the activity of God; therefore it would be *hubris* for us to claim mission for entirely ourselves. The Church is a creation of the Risen Christ and a servant of the kingdom or reign of God; therefore it would be preposterous for the Church to claim the initiative for mission. We ourselves, committed Christians, are *ministers:* servants, attendants, lesser functionaries—rather than as *magisters:* masters, teachers, major functionaries; therefore it would be arrogant to imagine that we are what clearly we are not.

Strictly speaking, the Church does not have a mission; rather, the mission has a Church. Strictly speaking, we do not have a mission; rather the mission has us, individually and collectively. If the Church will be Church, and if we will be who we are called and commissioned to be, then God can be God. The Church is not in charge of the mission anymore than we are in charge of it; God is in charge.

We are certainly right to believe that God chose or elected the Church as an instrument of mission, and that God chooses us, individually and collectively, as instruments of mission. Like the Church, we are simply called to be faithful, not to attempt to control the mission, or God. We are faithful when we respond to the call, when we are commissioned and sent: sent as laborers in the vineyard: sent to engage in and be faithful to collaborative ministry, whether with others—clerical or lay, male or female, from our own or another Christian tradition (or none), able-bodied or handicapped, willing or unwilling. We are sent, by God's grace and choice at this moment in history: therefore *the mission has us*. We must remain faithful. God will be God. The harvest is in God's hands.

RETURN TO PRAXIS

Practical theology insists that we begin with praxis, that we scrutinize and assess the appropriateness of the praxis, and that having reflected and analyzed, we return to a suitably modified praxis. Rosalee has been dead for over a decade now. But I have not forgotten her. The women at the shelter continue to choose, and to be grateful. And I continue to serve, but differently. The reflection in chapter 17 evokes, for me, the memory of Rosalee. If remembering is a way of keeping someone alive, then Rosalee still lives.

16

MEANING, FAITH, AND MINISTRY[1]

For decades, experts and diagnosticians have told us we are living between the times, amid paradigm shifts or breakdowns, and at the beginning of a new era (sometimes called *postmodernity,* sometimes confused with *globalization,* sometimes simply identified with the new millennium). Fluidity, change, chaos—and for too many people, meaninglessness and hopelessness—certainly mark our worlds of experience.

That provides a point of departure for a reflection on living meaningful, gospel-based lives, particularly focused on ministerial outreach to, and among, people at the margins of society. Yet a point of departure is no guarantee of a sure arrival. Nor does it necessarily indicate a clear direction to follow, much less an easy one. Perhaps that is why so many people feel bogged down, incapable of moving forward with determination, reduced to wandering aimlessly, or even overcome by a sense of futility.

This reflection is offered to anyone struggling with religion and faith, or with the tension of living between Church and kingdom. The operative word here is *struggling*; those beyond struggling, becalmed, or in a safe haven will find nothing of interest here. Nor are there guarantees for those who *are* struggling.

Taking the image of a journey (with its starting point, progress, and direction or orientation), the context of a storm (with its inclement conditions, and perhaps all-enveloping mist or fog), and the life-experience of a person of faith (with its ambiguity or messiness), I offer three suggestions. First, storms must not deter us; they are part of the natural (and supernatural) cycle. Second, lack of clarity about the outcome must not prevent our setting out and remaining committed; if life is *adventure* rather than merely a journey, we simply cannot know the outcome in advance; yet adventure is the very stuff of life. Third, we should be both steadfast and sensible, confusion or uncertainty notwithstanding: In order to proceed we need a compass, a compass bearing, and a sense of purpose. It is not enough to set out; we must be at least minimally equipped. The compass in this instance is our faith's (magnetic) core; the compass bearing is God's (magnetic) attraction; our sense of purpose is our commitment to the God who is always faithful.

I use *theological reflection* as the analogue of an effective compass, *homeless people* as a metaphorical needle to point us in the right direction, and *service* or *ministry* as our sense of purpose. But an expensive compass is of little help unless it can be read; the needle is not itself the way ahead but merely orients us and points in the right direction; and service can degenerate into self-indulgence. Many people have not learned to use a compass to orient their life's adventures; many have not discovered life's cardinal point, so they lack conviction; and innumerable good people have not (yet) discovered the rewards of service or ministry. It would be very sad, therefore, if we were to rail against the night or spend our lives in futility, when the instruments that could be most useful are actually within our reach.

THEOLOGICAL REFLECTION

"When we deliberately incorporate wisdom from our Christian heritage into the process of uncovering *the meanings* in our life-experiences, we are doing theological reflection."[2] Viktor Frankl identified *meaninglessness* as the greatest malaise of the Western world in the twentieth century, and the situation is no better today. In the so-called First World, millions of people do not know whether life has any meaning at all, or if so, what it might be. Theological reflection (to people of faith, and perhaps by contagion spreading more widely in society) provides an opportunity and a means for making sense of our lives. But it can do more: it can help to change lives. This is critically important for all who are committed to their own conversion and to serving others. The assertion that "you repent, not by feeling bad but by thinking different[ly]"[3] is pointedly apt. Theological reflection changes us by causing us to see, think, and act differently in our daily lives.[4] Dianne Bergant goes further: it is "aimed at human transformation, *of the faith community and the world*."[5]

Some people do theological reflection, many do not, yet everyone *could*; and everyone *should* if they are seriously committed to finding meaning by discovering discipleship and living their faith fully. But many Christians seem not to understand discipleship, nor to have an intimate relationship with God. So their faith cannot reach its potential and they themselves remain frustrated. So what *is* theological reflection, and how might it contribute?

Some people do theological reflection without naming it. Nevertheless, what is at implicit or informal can become intentional and more effective. Conversely, some people may claim that they are doing theological reflection though they never seem to develop its potential. Authentic theological reflection turns us both within (to focus us on our Christian heritage) and without (to engage with people and situations near, or just beyond our grasp). These are not two separate movements but an integrated process, analogous to breathing in and breathing out: each is essential to sustaining life.

Theological reflection is neither spiritual navel-gazing nor wishful thinking, but a concerted effort both to engage with processes that will change us and actually move us to undertake change in the world. It "enriches and challenges us on our journeys [adventures] in faith. It invites us to discern God's presence [compass bearing] and to move deeply into the world and not away from it" [following the compass bearing].[6] We are called to engage our lives and our Christian heritage from a standpoint of exploration, willing to *trust that God is present in our experience* and that our religious tradition has something to give us.[7]

When Christians vote with their feet (leaving the Church or discovering fundamentalism) there is acute need for understanding and creative dialogue. Many people seek meaning in their own Christian lives and in their engagement with the lives of others. Indeed, they sense that the former requires the latter: they look beyond themselves and their familiar ecclesial structures (local parishes turned in on themselves and dying by degrees) and attend to the needs of the wider world. Both these poles are significant: the wider world (in terms of needy persons), and the deeper desires of Christians themselves. They might be expressed as *outreach* and *inreach*.

Outreach moves us toward actual people: a case in point would be particular homeless people in our local shelters or subsisting on our streets; we should not merely acknowledge "the homeless" generically, but endeavor to encounter them in person. *Inreach* might be exemplified in the practice of theological reflection. Together, both processes may contribute to a rediscovery of personal meaning and provide the essential social dimension of our Christian lives. Such a combination can produce transformation and lead us back to a renewed praxis of ecclesial life, but charged now with a missionary spirit and the capacity both to challenge familiar ecclesial structures and to call local believing communities to conversion. Thomas Ogletree expresses this very well:

> To offer hospitality to the stranger is to welcome something new, unfamiliar, and unknown, into our life-world. Hospitality requires recognition of the stranger, vulnerability in an alien world; hospitality [also] designates

occasions of potential discovery, which can open up our narrow, provincial worlds. Strangers have stories to tell which we have never heard before, stories which can re-direct our seeing and our imaginations. The stories invite us to view the world from a novel perspective. The stranger does not simply challenge or subvert our assumed world of meaning; she may enrich, even transform, the world.[8]

The stories in part 1 should stand both as appropriate illustrations and as implicit invitations to anyone with willingness and imagination.

BECOMING VERSED IN THE ART

Fluency in theological reflection is enhanced by practice. Yet some theory is also necessary. Theological reflection requires us to bring individual and corporate experience into conversation with the wisdom of a religious heritage. Such conversation is a genuine dialogue that seeks mutual enrichment. Theological reflection therefore may *challenge, confirm, clarify, and expand* the way we understand both our experience and our tradition. The outcome is *new truth and meaning for living.*[9] The fruit is our ongoing conversion.

There are two prerequisites. First, a *tradition*: a heritage of accumulated and transmitted wisdom combining theology with practical and symbolic action. Second, a reservoir of *experience:* exposure to human encounters and the resulting personal modification. Theological reflection will engage Christians with the Jewish-Christian tradition, specifically the fundamental truths of faith and modes of action that are consistent with the person and teachings of Jesus.

There will be significant problems for Christians unfamiliar with the tradition, and for those whose Christianity remains virtually undeveloped since grade school. People who pick and choose what to believe or to do are unlikely to be attracted to theological reflection as a discipline. But Christians with a vague and nonlocalized sense of emptiness or meaninglessness may find theological reflection of immense assistance—provided they are serious about seeking a remedy.

Many "good Christians" have virtually no pastoral outreach or engagement. Though faithful in religious observances, and highly law-abiding citizens, they do not realize (in both senses) their baptism's potential: they have never developed a missionary spirit, an active and intimate prayer life, or a realization that they are called to a *developing* relationship with God. Without some level of intentional theological reflection they may never reach their potential. Some see no reason to change. Others feel they have nothing to learn from peers or forebears.

Lines of T. S. Eliot (their edge perhaps dulled by use) may still be a helpful stimulus here, and suggest a way forward:

> *We shall not cease from exploration*
> *And the end of all our exploring*
> *Will be to arrive where we started*
> *And know the place for the first time*
>
> LITTLE GIDDING, PT. 5

Here the operative word is *exploration*. Only those willing to move forward into unfamiliar territory, gathering accumulated *experience* and the *reflection* it has generated, become people of *wisdom*; only those who pursue wisdom will make authentic discoveries that produce *insight* to change their lives. Many Christians fail to explore their own faith or God's faithfulness; because of timidity or conceit they grow older but not wiser, observing religious conventions but without a deepening faith or a capacity for faith sharing, or an experience of the God who calls, sends, and sustains.

Exploration should mark our faith-lives. If it does, we will make discoveries that will not only illuminate the way ahead but help us to understand the significance of the way already traveled.

Explorers cannot anticipate the precise nature of their discoveries, but theological reflection will help us identify and interpret our *experience*, our actual encounters. But we must not overlook the *tradition*: study of the Christian story includes meditation on the call to discipleship. Sadly, many simply cannot find the time and space for discernment, prayer, and gaining insights about God's concern for their apparently petty lives. Perhaps they lack the imagination to find a different rhythm or take a different path: that requires close attention to local details and circumstances. Theological reflection is perfectly compatible with the routine or the humdrum, *if we make time for it.*

But there is a complementary perspective, afforded by deliberately engaging in some "vocational" pursuit. This too may enrich the lives of many.

HOMELESSNESS: SCANDAL ON OUR DOORSTEP

Signs of sinfulness and selfishness are all around, giving us pause as we proceed through life, not allowing us to point an accusing finger but challenging us to give an account of our own Christian stewardship in a bruised and needy world. We *are* our brother's [and sister's] keepers (Genesis 4:9). On Judgment Day we will know that whatever we did (or failed to do) to or for our least significant and most needy brothers and sisters is the measure of our response to or for Christ. Our social responsibilities are not optional.

Poor and needy people; men and women in prisons, hospitals and nursing homes; aged and housebound individuals; homeless, overlooked, forgotten and abandoned citizens; refugees, undocumented "aliens," and all manner of victims: these are only some of the faces of God that we so often ignore or fail to identify. They continue to suffer when we overlook them, while we fail to become who we are called to be. We must explore the edges of our comfortable worlds, make encounters, gain insights, come to deeper grasp of the meaning and purpose of our own lives, indelibly marked by baptism and by God's call and commission.

Patricia O'Connell Killen and John de Beer illustrate the potential of theological reflection by recounting the story of "Elaine," who herself worked in a shelter for homeless people. Their exposition can shape our own reflections, too. But voluntary work, or pastoral commitment, is virtually unlimited in shape and scope: the most important thing for would-be Christians is to look for *any* situation of need, and actually offer to do something to help. An element of risk is intrinsic to Christian discipleship. Yet the way of many Christians is paved only with good intentions, which accounts for our frequent failure to become the people of *The Way* of Jesus.

"Elaine" found herself tense and burdened after being at the shelter. But people vary, and we ourselves could be energized and liberated by such an experience of simple service, and recommitted to the Christian endeavor. Crucially, we should first *have* an experience, then *reflect* on it and discern what it might mean and point to: this is *insight,* which should lead to renewed *praxis.* But since the fruit of experience partly depends on our biases and presuppositions, we must carefully identify these. To repent by thinking and acting differently is a challenge for us all, but an attitude of exploration or adventure will make us more open to risk and transformation.[10] Our encounters will then not only take us back to previous personal experience, but (integrated with theological reflection) lead to a reexamination of our religious heritage as a repository of practical wisdom. This requires reading, learning, and prayerful integration, which many people are unwilling to invest in their Christian lives.

Indelible gospel images challenge us to venture out, to launch into the deep or to leave the boat and come to Jesus across the waves, but precisely when we would far prefer to remain in the shallows or hunker down in safety. If, as Christians, we recall that Christ calls *in order to send,* invites people to come *in order to commission* them to go, we might be willing to explore the implications of discipleship. We might recall too, the insightful comment that the "problem" with Christians is not the evil they do, individually or corporately, but the good they fail to do: Jesus said the kingdom was not for those who say "Lord, Lord," but for those who do God's will. That includes, beyond religious observance, a taste for God's own justice and commitment to God's own poor people, flesh-and-blood women and men. There is hardly a city in the United States in which homelessness is not a serious social problem—for its victims if not for the citizenship in general. Whatever we do or fail to do to the least, the forgotten, or the invisible, we do or fail to do to Christ himself.

To approach an unfamiliar social situation where help is needed is to take a step in the direction of our own conversion. Conversion is a process coextensive with life, through which we become *trans*formed or *re*formed and thus *con*formed to Christ. It implies change, and that can only happen if we are willing accomplices: if we *say* that we want to be more Christian, we must also undertake to be changed. If we undertake to be changed, we must also allow for new experiences in our lives. One kind of new experience is a consciously undertaken commitment to needy people: the *anawim,* God's poor.

We must then discover a "fit" or convergence between our good intentions and the legitimate needs of others. Sometimes we approach others only on our own terms: we know beforehand just what we are prepared to do. Then our service is a program rather than a discovery procedure; we take and maintain initiatives ourselves. Authentic ministry demands willingness to meet the needs of others. Thus the necessity of dialogical service, which requires reflection on how well our outreach reflects the Christian idea of service.

If we hold to what our faith teaches, we do not believe in generic creation: there are, we noted, no people *in general,* only actual, particular, individuals. "The poor" and "the homeless" are categories, abstractions. Concretely, we can only identify actual people. We cannot claim to be concerned *about,* much less *for* "the poor," unless we actually know some poor people, as Jesus did. To *know about,* that "outer knowledge," distinguished from to *know,* which is "inner knowledge"—that comes from encounter. On Judgment Day we will not pass muster by claiming to *know about* any number of things or problems: we will need to demonstrate that we have actually been acquainted with the grief of grieving people or the poverty of flesh-and-blood poor persons; that we have touched and been touched by real lives other than our own; that we have known the inner history of God's actual poor, needy or insignificant ones, some of whom we too know by name. Outreach to homeless people, or to actual members of any of the other social categories, is one proof that we take Christ and our faith seriously. Theological reflection based on such encounter is the warranty that our outreach is authentic, faith-based, and contributing to our own conversion.

"TO WHOM SHALL WE GO?"

Christian living is not vegetative existence or assimilation to the surrounding culture: it requires dialogue between our religious tradition and our life's experience. We start with the activity of our daily lives, perhaps recalling these words of Socrates: "The unexamined life is not worth living." But the examined life will result in change: in modification of experience so that it comes into greater conformity with the call of Christ. Commitment to social justice (a preferential option for actual poor persons) is the litmus test of a mature Christian life. A spirit of prudent risk and adventurous exploration might help us to respond to our calling, to remain faithful, and to use the God-given compass of our faith as we seek our true selves, and one another, and God. Theological reflection can help us to log and interpret our journeys and to keep us on track, whether by commitment to the homeless poor in our neighborhood or to other forgotten, victimized, or abandoned brothers and sisters. But we *must* reach out. We *must* go. We *must* extend the edges of our experience in order to enrich our theological reflection, and, with God's grace, to renew of the face of the earth. We *must* be on the way: on *The Way*. We need courage, clarity, and compass in order to reach the magnetic Pole. The time is now, the place is here, the person is each of us. With careful (theological) reflection and genuine (pastoral) experience, we will find the pearl, the treasure, the meaning of life: the realm of God.

17

MEALS, MEMORIES, AND PRACTICAL THEOLOGY[1]

G od gave us memory so that we might have roses in December." The words are from J. M. Barrie, creator of Peter Pan, and the whole phrase triggers in me the sweet pain of nostalgia. *Peter Pan* brings to mind Christmastime and a distant childhood afternoon in England, a fur-clad maiden aunt, a trip to the theater, and almost breathless excitement and wonder. "Roses in December" instantly evokes the harrowing and poignant documentary of four missionary women killed in El Salvador.[2] And memory is the thread that links us to other worlds, other times, other experiences.

THE POWER OF MEMORY

This chapter is shaped around a thought and an image. The thought is that memories are immensely powerful, certainly to hurt but also to heal. The image is that of Jesus saying insistently, "Do this in memory of me." Is it possible to bring these together and to weave a metaphor about nourishing, even "sacramental" memories? We can try, evoking memories of food and fellowship, and homelessness without helplessness or hopelessness.

It has been said that the young live in the future because they have no memories, while the old live in the past because they do. True or not, there is a strong association between human life and memory. Neurobiologists say it takes about three years for an experience to be lodged in the long-term memory,[3] a process that creates new synaptic pathways or significantly strengthens old ones. Memories are actually physical, brain-modifying realities. Under controlled electrical stimulation the brain yields its treasured memories, in verbal and emotional outpourings of great power.

According to Gilbert and Sullivan, "It's love that makes the world go round." Though less lyrical than love, memory may be just as significant. Memory acts like good lubricating oil, maintaining worlds of meaning in reasonable order and preventing them from seizing up. Without memory we would soon become incapable of moving forward purposefully.

We are well aware of the memory-destroying potential of certain drugs or strokes, and of the ravages of Alzheimer's disease: people without recallable memories are isolated from others and become withdrawn, imprisoned within a private world. We may also be aware of the prodigious memories of certain people and the way in which their ability to tap into their memory-store allows them to connect with their wider community, to relive events and thereby strengthen their social links, and actually to maintain their community's identity over time.[4] The ability to remember and share stories is a precious social skill and a significant cultural trait among people who cherish their communal identity and common destiny.

MEMORIES AND SURVIVAL

Among this nation's homeless poor (whose numbers stand as a silent indictment of a prosperous, self-absorbed, and perhaps *culpably forgetful* society) are people touched by mental illness or suffering from drug abuse. They have been so badly victimized or traumatized that some of their memories are buried forever. Other memories are too painful to recall, while yet others lie frozen like a body within a glacier, never to be touched by the life-giving warmth of nostalgia. Then there are those so-called "street people," perhaps limited in social skills or native intelligence, who appear to use their memories as the very home they lack: memories form a cozy cabin into which they withdraw for the duration of a never-ending winter. People who seek to retreat in this way smile vacantly—or look out sightlessly on a world to whose icy blasts they are quite impervious.

But there are many other people, also living on the streets of our cities, whose memories are virtually their only negotiable currency, their sole possession, and certainly the only one beyond the reach of violent or thieving hands. Memories are their legacy and treasure. These are the people who, though by no means immune from maudlin recollections, know that the controlled rekindling of the embers of memory can warm their hearts, reminding them of who they are, because who they are is so intimately connected with who they used to be. For such fire-hardened souls, the loneliness and isolation of the daily struggle may be tempered and even assuaged by the memories that link them with those they have loved and those who have loved them. Their names are legion: Tina, Brenda, Darla, Deborah…

To recall the therapeutic value of memories is not to romanticize the lives of people who remember. For among the deep-furrowed synapses there is also anger and rage, dashed hopes and broken dreams; and sometimes these passions breed in the dark. But there can be a healing value as well: memories can be, in a real sense, redemptive, as we have seen in part 1. Those of us who are privy to them can hardly fail to have been both appalled and deeply moved.

Memory and the Christian Story

"Do this in memory of me," said Jesus. Gregory Dix, in his monumental work on the liturgy, asks rhetorically:

> Was ever another command so obeyed? For century after century, spreading slowly to every continent and country and among every race on earth, this action has been done, in every conceivable human circumstance, for every conceivable human need.[5]

Lyrical though this passage is as it builds, reaches its crest, and rolls majestically on, it leaves a number of questions in its wake. What is "this action" of which Dix speaks? What indeed is the "this" which Jesus commands us to do in his memory? And what is the relation between an action, a memory, and a life?

If we have restricted the memorializing (*anamnesis*) of Jesus to a particular action (even to the eucharistic action, the liturgy), we may have seriously failed to understand the nature and power of memory, both in the theological sense of *anamnesis* and in the existential experience of men and women. For what is the "this" to which Jesus referred, if not *his whole life*, gathered up, summarized, epitomized, and presented in concentrated form in his action at the Last Supper? We are bidden, surely, to do what Jesus did: not simply to break bread and share drink, or to be fed around a table, but to be with, to become like, and to be animated by, the Spirit of Jesus. We are called—as he was—to be the seed that falls to the ground, dies, and rises in the fresh and nourishing food that is given for all. This is what Eucharist really means, what it really entails. Like Jesus, we are called and sent so that we will be picked, pressed and poured out for others in the thirst-quenching draught that restores parched lives and drooping spirits. We are called in order to be sent, and to be raised up, exploited, belittled or despised. Only when we begin to grasp this and try and live it, are we truly attempting to do "this" in memory of Jesus.

To remember someone is to bring them alive in our mind and emotions. The opposite of remembering is forgetting (or dis-membering: brutalized Brenda is remembered and restored to the community whenever we bring her to mind). To be completely forgotten by everyone is to die: to suffer social death. Societies that venerate ancestors acknowledge a special category of those who remain alive in the memory of the living. When the last link with the living memory is cut, a deceased person is either retired into the ranks of the undifferentiated dead or is remembered as an exceptional person, a named hero or founder, through litanies recited on special occasions.

The communion of saints is the remembered community of those who have gone before us, marked with the sign of faith: our ancestors whose memory we cherish and keep alive. Jesus invites us to keep his memory alive, to keep him as a living part of our lives and experience. So long as there is even one of us alive to bring him to mind, to remember him, actively to represent his life (not only through formal liturgy but through all authentic *anamnesis*) and to craft our own lives according to his, then he truly lives in our lives and he can participate in "every conceivable circumstance" of those lives.

If we think that "this" (the liturgical form) has already been done "in every conceivable human circumstance," we are far from understanding the lives and the rights of the poor and the outcasts of this land: those without parish or faith-community, those without hearth or home.

STAYING ALIVE

A shelter for homeless people is no place for formal liturgy, for Eucharist. But it may be a place where hope is kept alive and memories are created and evoked. Indeed, unless it serves, in some way, to nourish memories and spirits as well as bodies, it lacks true humanness. If the dynamic "calling to mind" of Jesus is true religion and a real expression of ministry, perhaps the actual making of memories can also be an act of faith, an expression of hope, a symbol of charity. It is in this spirit that every Friday morning over many winters,[6] a hot and nourishing, simple yet varied, breakfast was served to and shared with and among those homeless women who spent Thursday night at the shelter.

If theology must speak to real people or fall mute; if theology that fails to speak justice and hope is a booming gong or a clashing cymbal; and if every theology is a local theology, there has to be an appropriately graced means of reminding people (literally "in every conceivable human circumstance") of their dignity, potential, and worth. Some homeless poor people in Chicago have learned, have remembered, that there is a "special" breakfast just for them on Fridays. It is special, not so much because it is lavish (which it is not) but because it is assured, fresh, nourishing, appropriate—and it comes with *table service.*

Most meals eaten by homeless people are obtained only after waiting in line. This weekly breakfast is special because it is brought to the table where the women are seated *as normal people usually are.* It is special, in the women's view, because it is identifiable as real table-sharing, table-fellowship. It is a kind of communion. And over the years—though slowly and only by degrees— the women who stay at the shelter on Thursday nights have become noticeably more mellow and less strident or aggressive. Seated together at table and waited on, they are in turn more likely to pass the condiments than to stretch for what they want. They are getting used to being treated with courtesy by those around them and are more inclined to use words rusty with disuse: "Thank you," "I enjoyed that," and even some superlatives. The communion leaves its mark.

After a decade of Friday breakfasts, many of the women moved on or passed on. Yet for most, their sojourn in the shelter was certainly long enough for them to form a memory: a memory of Friday mornings, of the smell of bacon and pancakes, of smiles and gentle words, and of forgotten people gathered around a common table. It would be a memory composed of taking, eating, drinking, and sharing, a memory of temporary peace and of fragile bonding. If the memory evoked in the minds of some reminds them nostalgically of Eucharist, perhaps others are content simply to remember an almost forgotten time of nourishment, of give and take, and of enough food for everyone: actually, there really is not too much to choose between them.

As a eucharistic people, gathered at our own various tables, we are promised a blessing if we are hungry and thirsty *for justice, for righteousness* (Matthew 5:6). The action of Jesus and its memory needs to reach out to hallow "every conceivable human circumstance" of our lives and the lives we touch. We are called to commit ourselves to seeking appropriate, graced responses to "every human need." We are invited to create healing and nourishing memories for people who have been overlooked, forgotten, and swallowed up in abstract categories: "the outcast," "the homeless," and "the poor." We are challenged to make sure that there will always be roses for as long as there is December.

18

REVELATION AND RESPONSIBILITY

Insofar as religion has to do with knowledge (of facts, expectations, rules, sanctions, and so on), it is largely a matter of *knowing about.* "Religious knowledge" teaches us about God, about doctrine and dogma, about orthodoxy (belief) and orthopraxis (behavior). It can be rather complicated; even dull.

In many ways, faith is much simpler than religion. Faith is also about knowing but not *knowing about.* Faith is simply *knowing:* knowing experientially, knowing by experience or familiarity. The object of religious faith is God. Saint Paul says, "I *know* in whom I have believed." We can know God without seeing God, because God is knowable in many ways, including in our neighbors, including the homeless poor. Faith is the commitment to, the perseverance in a relationship with the God we have not seen as clearly as we might like, but whom nevertheless we *know.*

Part 1 offered a glimpse of the "inner history" of homelessness. The women spoke directly of what they know, what they have encountered and experienced firsthand; they speak for themselves. We can read, hear, and attempt to understand, but we cannot experience their experience. Part 2 has tried to articulate the "outer history" ("knowing about" homelessness vicariously), as a way to awake our consciousness, to make us more aware of our responsibilities to our neighbors. This supplementary information is intended to stimulate reflection and lead to action: to a renewed *praxis* of Christian ministry.

WOMEN'S FAITH: A REVELATION

Revelation is what God wants to disclose and how God wants to be known: it is available to everyone, everywhere.[1] It is God's constant and cosmic self-giving and self-disclosure. Religion, by contrast, is what people (culturally, institutionally, denominationally) actually *make of* Revelation. It is whatever they grasp of God's mighty manifestation. But since we are human and finite, whatever we are able to grasp is nevertheless only partial, incomplete. No one, no religion, can grasp the unsearchable riches of God. Religion is essentially a human (cultural) creation. At its best, religion mirrors quite well what God wants to reveal; at its worst, it can be a distorting mirror, an insupportable burden for its adherents, or even a tragic misunderstanding of what God is trying to reveal. Every religion remains in constant need of purification, the better to reflect and underwrite God's Revelation.

Though religion (particularly as formalized in the great monotheisms: Judaism, Christianity, Islam) postulates a faith-relationship between Creator and creature, many "religious" people fail to develop that relationship. Religious observance alone may establish creaturely dependence on the Creator, but this may become a relationship of codependency or nonreciprocity rather than one that is mutual and life-giving. The result is either formalism (rule-keeping without vital and responsible living) or the eventual abandonment of religious observance as irrelevant or oppressive.

Homeless women may be more or less religious: most I know were raised in a religious environment. Some still find sustenance in religious observance and church attendance. But many are not churchgoers, or only sporadically so. Large numbers of those who once frequented churches feel betrayed or duped by the established church, and some are no longer religious in a conventional sense. But I never met a homeless woman without faith.

If faith is measured by commitment and trust rather than by palpable rewards or success in one's ventures, it may actually help homeless people to survive. Faith carried into tomorrow and the next day is what we mean by hope. This book tries to illustrate that where there's hope, there's life. Without hope, life ceases to have meaning, and survival becomes so difficult as to sometimes be not even desirable. Half a century ago, Viktor Frankl argued that when life is really difficult, those who survive will be the people with something to live for: and most often, *something* translates into *someone*. He noted that a survivor of World War II with no one left in the world found it far more difficult to survive than one who had lost many family or friends but who still felt loved by someone—or had discovered a focus in life: someone to love or to serve. Then life, however difficult and fraught, became bearable and livable.

The *someone* many homeless women have to live for is a child, a lover, or (less commonly) a spouse. But also, for virtually all these women, the *someone* is also the God they know and trust. It is in God they put their faith. They may not be recognizably religious, but their faith is fierce.

Themes and Variations

Reflecting on these stories and these lives, five themes seem to recur with some frequency. They are perhaps the bedrock on which these women's survival is built. As such, they bear reflection. They may have lessons for us.

First and foremost is this strong and resilient faith, which is not necessarily (in fact quite rarely) manifest in conventional religious observance nor in the adherence to beliefs (formalized propositions intended to test orthodoxy). What is evident and perhaps surprising is how many women live by faith sustained by personal prayer and even conversation with God.

The second theme is really embedded in the first: the women have no doubt about the reality of God. They are not searching for faith—though they may be more or less curious about religious belonging and about further knowledge of Scripture. What they already have, quite palpably, is "inner knowledge" of God: they know God in some profound and personally convincing sense. What they may not have, *and appear not to need*, is an increased "outer knowledge"—knowledge about God, or Church, Scripture or beliefs. They may be said to have spirituality rather than religion, and faith rather than belief. But it is recognizably monotheistic, if not explicitly Christian, and the God is clearly the God of Abraham, Isaac, and Jacob. Only once did I meet a woman who claimed to believe in a god widely different from the God I recognize: she said she was a kind of Jewish Buddhist, and she seemed to find that entirely appropriate.

Third: in very many cases, Jesus is a shadowy or less relevant figure than "God"—who is identified as spirit, Spirit, or even a generalized sense of peacefulness. Initially, it was surprising to discover that Jesus did not occupy center stage. But having heard horror stories about how men have brutalized and betrayed these women, it became much less surprising: perhaps they simply cannot relate to Jesus as man, as male. Maybe they need a relationship (to God) without such heavy personal overtones.

The fourth characteristic is no less striking than the others: despite personal suffering, tragedy, and heartbreak, the women are virtually unanimous in not blaming God. Listening to their stories was a vivid reminder of years ago, exchanging conventional greetings with and among the Mende people of Sierra Leone. The expected response to the expected question, "How is the body" [how are you]? was "There is no blame on God" or "There is nothing to blame God for." Some might call this a superstitious or fearful reaction: if one were to blame God, perhaps even worse things would befall! But among Mende people and homeless women alike, it is anything but that: it reminds them not to curl up and die, not to give up the struggle, but to do the best they can and continue to have faith in God's providence.

This ties neatly with the final common thread running through the women's testimony: their abiding hope. Again, it is easy to say that if they gave up hope they would be overwhelmed. But they do not simply cling semiconsciously to hope: they embrace it fiercely and passionately, refusing to abandon trust in a sometimes distant and silent God. In their hope is their life. All who hope continue to live. All who abandon hope effectively abandon life.

LESSONS TOO LATE FOR THE LEARNING?

This faith-without-Jesus is a challenge to conventional Christians, especially pastors and ministers. It leaves me thinking two kinds of thoughts. The first is about our language and preaching; the second is about our ministry and outreach.

As far as language is concerned, if we insist on Jesus, or simply take Jesus for granted in our thinking and preaching, do we "reduce" or "confine" God? If we talk only of Jesus, our words may be irrelevant to some people, or they may alienate, as some of the women's stories indicate. Still, most women like those who talked with me simply do not come to church services. What would happen if we were to integrate the God of the Old Testament more? Might we not struggle more consciously with God as Trinity, as well as with both the transcendent (Father, Spirit) and immanent (Jesus, Christ) aspects of divinity? Would not this challenge our thinking and preaching in a creative way? How and when do we talk of the Spirit who is God, or God the Creator— in the back streets, dark alleys, and "projects" of whose creation our homeless people subsist?

As for ministry, what if more of us left the security and familiarity of the church buildings and ventured into the streets in search of God, or images of God, and of other people's encounters with God? In an era where Church congregations are hemorrhaging, might not the faith-reflections of homeless women (not to mention young people, incarcerated prisoners or the throngs of the "faithful, departed") stimulate us to new pastoral responses and initiatives? Might not a renewal of outreach provide a renewal of our own apostolic lives?

Christians and Christianity should be "exocentric," not "endocentric," turned inside-out rather than outside-in, everted rather than inverted. Christianity exists for mission and not for maintenance. Unless we move out, reach out, and encounter, we will wither on the vine. We are gathered precisely so that we may be scattered in the name of Jesus. We have been called in order to be sent to our brothers and sisters whom we have not yet seen. But this is not a matter of "us" giving and "them" receiving: it is a matter of mutuality. We are mutually indebted to one another. Each of us has something we can share. By doing so, all are enriched, God is praise, and the kingdom or realm of God is just a little closer than before.

OCTOBER 2, 2005
ANNIVERSARY OF THE DEATH OF CLAUDE FRANÇOIS POULLART DES PLACES,
FOUNDER, CONGREGATION OF THE HOLY GHOST (SPIRITANS) 1679–1709,
BETHLEHEM, REPUBLIC OF SOUTH AFRICA

NOTES

Introduction

1. Even more frequently, people are further demeaned and depersonalized by being referred to as "prostitutes" rather than *women* (in prostitution), or "the homeless" rather than *persons* (or homeless *women* or *men*), and so on.

2. In the *Journal of the International Association of Mission Studies* (1988): 141–144. Paul Jenkins outlines an approach to mission history that would take oral traditions as seriously as written ones. But such an approach requires the development of new ways of retrieving, recording, and evaluating that tradition.

3. Ranger, Terence O. and John Weller, eds., *Themes in the Christian History of Central Africa* (Berkeley: University of California Press, 1975).

4. Pickens, George F., "The 'God Talk' of an African Christian Patriarch: The Formation and Presentation of Matthew Ajuoga's Johera Narrative." Ph.D. Dissertation (United Kingdom: University of Birmingham, 1997), 169, 205.

5. For the sake of simplicity, we hereafter refer only to "inner" and "outer" history or story.

6. Cohen, Anthony P., *Self Consciousness: An Alternative Anthropology of Identity* (London and New York: Routledge, 1994).

7. Cohen, *Self Consciousness*, 185–5.

8. The conclusion to the story of Tina Jackson (chapter 1) represents the follow-up interview.

9. I belong to the Congregation of the Holy Ghost, or Spiritans.

10. Ranger and Weller, eds., *Themes in the Christian History of Central Africa*, 3.

11. Burns, Robert, *To a Louse*, 1786.

12. Anthropologists have produced excellent material through "participant observation." However, it can be so highly theorized as to be unreadable to many people. Systematic or comprehensive treatment can be found in works such as Robert DeJarlais, *Shelter Blues: Sanity and*

Selfhood Among the Homeless (Philadelphia: University of Pennsylvania Press, 1997). Part 1 of this book is intended for the general reader: there is a minimum of theorizing. I edited the women's stories, but only in the interest of fluency and readability of narrative.

13. Stark, Rodney, *The Rise of Christianity: How the Obscure, Marginal Jesus Movement Became the Dominant Religious Force in the Western World in a Few Centuries* (Princeton, N.J.: Princeton University Press, 1996), 212.

14. The women's ages are given as of the time of the initial interview. Interviews took place over several years.

15. See chapter 17, "Meals, Memories, and Practical Theology."

16. Wiebe, Rudy, *The Blue Mountains of China* (Toronto: McClelland and Stewart,1970), 215–6.

17. Barbour, Claude-Marie, "Seeking Justice and Shalom in the City," *International Review of Mission* (1984): 303–309; John Boberg, "The Missionary as Anti-Hero," *Missiology* (1979): 411–421.

Chapter 1: Tina

1. The women at the shelter are expected to take advantage of a case manager, a qualified social worker employed by the organization (REST: Residents for Emergency Shelter Transitions) that runs the women's and men's shelters, as well as a drop-in center and other support systems. If a woman is working with a case manager, she will be helped to find a residence, usually a single-room occupancy (SRO) in a building dedicated to such housing, or perhaps a "transients' motel."

2. This presents the classic dilemma for people on disability: whether to find secure housing but not be able to afford to eat and take care of oneself, or to eat but not be able to afford rent. Thus many people in such circumstances find themselves in shelters, even though they are receiving some financial assistance: it simply is not enough to live on

Chapter 2: Jeanette

1. Women are thereby eligible for small privileges, and assistance from professional social workers.

2. Sarah's Circle is a drop-in center and safe house, for women, run by women, and exclusive to women. Uptown Ministries and Harper House are church-based outreach programs. Volunteering in places such as these can be a way for a homeless person to survive: volunteers receive food, clothing, and a degree of self-respect.

3. Jeanette spoke of three programs she had been in: NA, AA, and CA (Narcotics, Alcoholics, and Cocaine Anonymous).

4. The Northmere and the Sheridan are well-know—or notorious—SROs (single-room occupancy facilities). They represent transitional housing,

but have an air of decay and depression. Whenever I went to the *Northmere*, I was aware of feeling alienated and strange. I knew that I was identified as obviously "out of place" by the residents.

Chapter 3: Lunette

1. The shelters are single-sex, so Lunette and her son are split up, although the men's shelter is only a couple of blocks away: enough to ensure that they are really not together.
2. The women—and the men, for that matter—were let out of the shelter by 7:00 AM irrespective of weather. They could not congregate near, or return to the shelter before 8:00 PM, so the prospects were bleak and terrifying for anyone who had not yet learned some "street smarts."
3. But not necessarily enough to afford her own place, though Lunette is thrifty, and with her son's income can scrape together enough to dream about an apartment, which is more than many can do.
4. No questions asked, so long as she is "in good standing" with the REST authorities: that she is attending meetings, consulting with a social worker, or actively pursuing her own housing. Lunette qualifies for shelter residence because she does not need to attend meetings and she is seeking housing. The lottery refers to a nightly opportunity whereby some women who are not yet in programs or do not yet have a card may be admitted to the shelter, depending on availability of space (the shelter is only licensed to take forty-five per night) and the track record of the women themselves.

Chapter 4: Brenda

1. Not the women's shelter I frequent, since it does not cater to babies or children. Brenda and I met much later, when more damage had been done, and when her life was at a turning point.
2. "Notorious" is the only appropriate epithet for this public-housing project. It was one of the best known and badly reputed of all the projects. It was finally razed to the ground.
3. Genesis House was founded in 1984 by Edwina Gateley. In the earliest days, Depaul, OFM, Judy, OP, and Ted, a Canadian lay volunteer, were its residential core.
4. The poignancy of this projection will become clear in due course.
5. Brenda *must* try to supplement SSI in order to "get a life"; but if she is found out, she will be penalized, stands to lose her SSI, and will be in even worse straits.
6. Darla, Brenda's companion, is also the primary caregiver for two of Brenda's children!
7. Not having a card that assures her of a place in the shelter, Brenda has to chance the "lottery" in hopes of a bed. The number of lottery winners

depends each night on the number of beds still available after the cardholders have been admitted. But since Brenda wants to do day labor, she needs a decent night's sleep. Unless she can win a lottery place at the REST shelter, she is better off at another shelter where she has a better chance of a bed, even though it is not among friends or as close to her daily work. *Every day she must choose.*

8. My contribution is to cook a meal of fresh food, for the forty-five women who come to the shelter. The irony is that the women know exactly when I am due, and more women than usual will congregate at the Shelter. Thus, more than usual will be turned away. People like Brenda like to help peel potatoes, and this can sometimes get them into the shelter and secure a place for the night!

9. The Northmere is a single-room occupancy facility, with whose proprietors the REST Management has an arrangement. However, women only get a room if they are approved by REST, which means that they are in appropriate programs and receiving appropriate counseling. Brenda, a recidivist, ultimately lost her privileges, was expelled from the Northmere, and had to start again at the beginning, seeking to move from hoping for a bed (the lottery) to becoming a card holder again, and thus assured of a bed.

Chapter 6: Ranita

1. I neither concealed nor flaunted my clerical identity. The women wanted my name, not my professional status.

2. Ranita is comparing opportunities and prospects at the shelter with what she knows is available elsewhere. She is objectively correct, but REST does run a number of programs, and offers a broad range of opportunities consistent with its resources, both financial and personnel.

3. In the 1980s the Reagan Administration reclassified tens of thousands of "mentally sick" people, deinstitutionalizing them within a very short time. While this appealed to some liberal minds, it was both superficial and highly detrimental to many people who simply did not have the practical skills required for personal survival. Many of them gravitated toward shelters, where they received short-term assistance. What they needed was long-term care.

4. This was the first indication of family educational problems, or of Ranita's relative giftedness.

5. The context is the offices of the REST organization, and Penny is one of the women in line for her mail, or to make an appointment.

6. Ranita is in an SRO facility. She is remarking that seven of the women who were formerly in the shelter have "made it" into independent living. She could be suggesting that someone might hire her in the capacity of a resident assistant or counselor.

Chapter 7: Lynette

1. The Department of Children and Family Services [DCFS] typically intervenes if the family unit is seriously compromised, or when an underage child is not under adequate parental or school control. The problems to which Lynette refers are largely those DCFS had with her, not vice versa.
2. A total of seven. But Lynette said that one was in California. Something is not quite right here.
3. This conversation took place at the very end of 1999.
4. Chapter 13 looks more closely at Church and God.

Chapter 8: Lisa

1. The reference to a thirty-two degree Mason trips very naturally off Lisa's tongue. The *Scottish Rite* awards thirty-two higher degrees of membership (the normal is three). But *Ancient Arabic Order of the Nobles of the Mystic Shrine* are "Thirty-second degree Masons," otherwise known as "the Shriners, noted for their colorful parades and support of children's hospitals." *The Columbia Encyclopedia*, sixth edition (New York: Columbia University Press, 2001–2005), 200: 1045.
2. Mrs. Crockett is Lunette [see chapter 3].

Chapter 9: Janet

1. Janet is a big woman: heavy-set, verging on the obese. I sensed she was aware of the resemblance, not only when she met her mother but when she was retelling the story for me. Another intimation of mortality, perhaps. Another mark of the hand of fate.
2. Today she will get five dollars as well as doughnuts. She does not need to demean herself for this: she has earned it.

Chapter 10: Deborah

1. This interview took place in 1999, so Deborah, born in 1964, would have been about thirty-five years old.

Chapter 11: Janice

1. As mentioned, the women knew that I would arrange a funeral for anyone in need, and for many, this was extremely important: they would not die unknown or unmourned. But I was out of town. The pastor of the Uptown Baptist Church was highly respected by many of the women, and evidently did a fine pastoral job.

Chapter 12: Lorraine

1. This was due to the much publicized "Welfare Reforms" of President Bill Clinton. They may well have stimulated some people to seek work, but they almost crushed people like Lorraine.
2. An important service provided by organizations like Sarah's Circle is to provide a *poste restante*, an address for people without permanent housing.
3. As with all the women's stories, the "God" conversation is the subject of chapter 13.

Chapter 14: Homeless Women and Popular Piety

1. This chapter originally appeared as "Faith, Piety, and Non-Institutional Christianity: Popular Religion Among Homeless Women," in *New Theology Review* (May 2000): 38–48.
2. Pope Paul VI, *Evangelii Nuntiandi*, §63, 1975.
3. "Pontifical Council for Culture," *Origins* (June 17, 1999): 65, 67–84.
4. *National Coalition for the Homeless*, June 1999.
5. This is not to forget that excellent church programs do exist.
6. For a review of the language, see Cristián Parker, *Popular Religion and Modernization in Latin Amercia: A Different Logic* (Maryknoll, NY: Orbis Books, 1996); Thomas Bamat and Jean-Paul Wiest, eds., *Popular Catholicism in a World Church: Seven Case Studies in Inculturation* (Maryknoll, N.Y.: Orbis Books, 1999).
7. Writing in *The Tablet*, May 8, 2004, A.N. Wilson avers that "the majority of decent people today find Christianity itself, whatever its coloring, impossible to believe" (27). This would characterize the Christian religion rather than the faith: an important distinction.
8. Rodriguez-Holguin, Jeanette Y. "Hispanics and the Sacred." Chicago Studies, August, 1990: 137–152. She uses the work of J.L. Gonzalez, "La Religiosidad popular desde la práctica de la liberación," in Iglesia y Religión, 16. Juarez, Mexico, 1983.
9. Bellah, Robert N., "Reforming Our Institutions of Meaning," in *Fugitive Faith: Interviews by Benjamin Webb* (Maryknoll, N.Y.: Orbis Books, 1998), 3–14.
10. Johnson, Elizabeth, "A Community of Holy People in a Sacred World: Rethinking the Communion of Saints." *New Theology Review* (May, 1999): 5–16.
11. These quotations are taken from the interviews with the women introduced in part 1.

Chapter 15: Practicing Collaborative Ministry

1. This chapter originally appeared as "Partners in God's Business: Mission as Collaborative Ministry," *Spiritan Studies* 10 (2000): 3–14.
2. Inculturation is the outcome of the engagement between the Gospel and a particular culture of community. The mature outcome will be a renewal of the community in terms of faith, hope, and love—and the exemplifications of those theological virtues in daily life and action.
3. The surprising and distressing document, *Dominus Iesus* took a giant step in the opposite direction. "Declaration '*Dominus Iesus*': On the Unicity and Salvific Universality of Jesus Christ and the Church," Congregation of Doctrine and Faith (CDF), 2000.
4. Bosch, David, *Transforming Mission: Paradigm Shifts in the Theology of Mission* (Maryknoll, N.Y.: Orbis Books, 1991), 10.
5. Ibid., 370.
6. Bevans, Stephen B., "Forty Years of Ecclesiology: From a Church with a Mission to a Mission with a Church." Unpublished.
7. Ibid.

Chapter 16: Meaning, Faith, and Ministry

1. This chapter originally appeared as "Searching for Meaning, Struggling for Faith: Pastoral Outreach and Theological Reflection" in *New Theology Review* (May 2004): 16–24.
2. Killen, P. O'Connell and John de Beer, *The Art of Theological Reflection* (New York: Crossroad, 1995), 46 (emphasis added).
3. Wiebe, Rudy, *The Blue Mountains of China* (Toronto: McClelland and Stewart, 1970), 216.
4. Killen and de Beer, *The Art of Theological Reflection*, 68
5. Bergant, Dianne, "Theological Reflection at Catholic Theological Union." Position Paper, Doctor of Ministry, 2002 (emphasis added).
6. Killen and de Beer, *The Art of Theological Reflection*, 76.
7. Ibid., 142.
8. Ogletree, Thomas W., *Hospitality to the Stranger: Dimensions of Moral Understanding* (Westminster: John Knox Press, 1985).
9. Killen and de Beer, *The Art of Theological Reflection*, viii (emphasis added).
10. Ibid., 47–51.

Chapter 17: Meals, Memories, and Practical Theology

1. This chapter initially appeared as a reflection: "The Memory Lingers On" in *New Theology Review* (August 1993): 81–85.
2. *Roses in December* is a documentary by Ann Carrigan (New York: First-Run Features, 1982).
3. Fox, Robin, "The Diversity of Anthropology and the Unity of Mankind: An Introduction to the Concept of Ethosystem," in *Waymarks*, edited by Kenneth Moore (Notre Dame, Ind.: University of Notre Dame Press, 1987), 17–42.
4. Lord, Albert B., *The Singer of Tales* (Cambridge, Mass.: Harvard University Press, 1960).
5. Dix, Gregory, *The Shape of the Liturgy* (San Francisco: Harper and Row, 1982), 744.
6. Chronologically, this chapter should have come before some of the others. After the mid-1990s (as explained earlier), the shelter discontinued the practice of serving a cooked breakfast, because there were now no overnight volunteers. The cooked breakfast has been replaced, symbolically, by our weekly cooked evening meal—surely no less eucharistic than its early morning counterpart.

Chapter 18: Revelation and Responsibility

1. See Vincent Donovan, *The Church in the Midst of Creation* (Maryknoll, N.Y.: Orbis Books, 1989), particularly 84–95.